I0820543

Your Intuitive Nudge

About the Author

Eboni Banks is an intuitive, survivor, writer, author, and embodied teacher as an intuition coach and intuitive healing mentor. She has been aware of her intuition since childhood and considers herself a mystic, as she enjoys exploring the balance of physical and non-physical life. She is also a certified yoga teacher and yoga nidra instructor, and she paints in her spare time. She lives in New York City, where she shares her spiritual work with clients. Visit her at BodyWayIntuition.com.

Your Intuitive Nudge

A Step-by-Step Guide to Connecting *with* Your Intuition

Eboni Banks

Woodbury, Minnesota

First Edition
First Printing, 2025

Book design by Samantha Peterson
Cover design by Shannon McKuhen
Interior illustrations by Llewellyn Art Department

Library of Congress Cataloging-in-Publication Data (Pending)
ISBN: 978-0-7387-7925-6

Llewellyn Publications
A Division of Llewellyn Worldwide Ltd.
2143 Wooddale Drive
Woodbury, MN 55125-2989
www.llewellyn.com

Printed in the United States of America

GPSR Representation:
UPI-2M PLUS d.o.o., Medulićeva 20, 10000 Zagreb, Croatia,
matt.parsons@upi2mbooks.hr

Forthcoming Books by Eboni Banks

Copy the Sky: A Memoir on Harmonizing Dark & Light

To intuition: Thank you for
nurturing my faith as I humbly
surrender to your living grace.

Contents

Exercises

EXERCISES

Introduction

MANY OF US ARE familiar with the phrase "We are spiritual beings having a human experience." However, few of us keep digging past the surface to uncover the dazzling nugget of golden wisdom contained within those words: The spiritual and physical aspects of us are in a continuous relationship, communicating through non-physical and physical expressions. Non-physical relates to the eternal, invisible world of the Spirit, while the physical refers to the temporary, visible world we experience as humans. Your body influences both aspects of your existence. It is the connection between your non-physical and physical aspects, which is a natural part of the human experience, enabling self-communication through intuition, making intuition a practical, present, and tangible part of daily life. For that reason, you are already using intuition whether you know it or not. It's impossible not to, as intuition is constant and inescapable, happening all day, every day. Actively using intuition is a spiritual practice that empowers you to appreciate yourself and your ability to manage the ongoing relationship between your spiritual and physical aspects and, ultimately, your relationship with yourself. Embracing your intuition is a recognition of self that enhances your belief in your capacity to experience spiritual life.

A Bit About This Book

If you are new to intuition, this book serves as more than just an introduction. If you are already familiar with intuition, regardless of how little or how much, you will still find plenty of new insights to take away. Experiencing intuition for yourself is key (and what this book is all about) because, like anything, the experience starts with befriending it. This book provides tools to help you experience more of your intuition by enhancing your awareness of yourself and your connection with the world around you. Throughout the text, you will learn how intuition communicates with you and how to effectively harness your intuition to benefit all areas of your life. The book is highly personal and designed for your unique journey of self-discovery, as understanding intuition is highly individualized. Your countless individual experiences with intuition will vary and depend on how open you are to experiencing life differently.

Each step is a set of actionable tools to carry with you for the rest of your life, making this book a valuable resource for personal growth. In addition to the writings, you'll find intuitive exercises to practice on your own and at your own pace, reminders, real-life intuition stories, self-love actions, suggested journal prompts, and quotes to repeat aloud, giving your entire system a new command. These interactive components also serve as a practical resource to capture your thoughts, feelings, experiences, and actions as you explore and learn more about your intuition and how to engage it.

The resources in this book are helpful companions on your journey of self-exploration, reinforcing your learning as you delve deeper into who you are: a spiritual being having a human experience.

The Chakras

To add a layer of support in aligning with your non-physical self, chapters 2 through 8 end with a chakra exercise that correlates with one of the seven main chakras. Chakras are non-physical, round, disc-like whirls of energy located inside the physical body. The seven main chakras are located in specific places in the body along the spine.

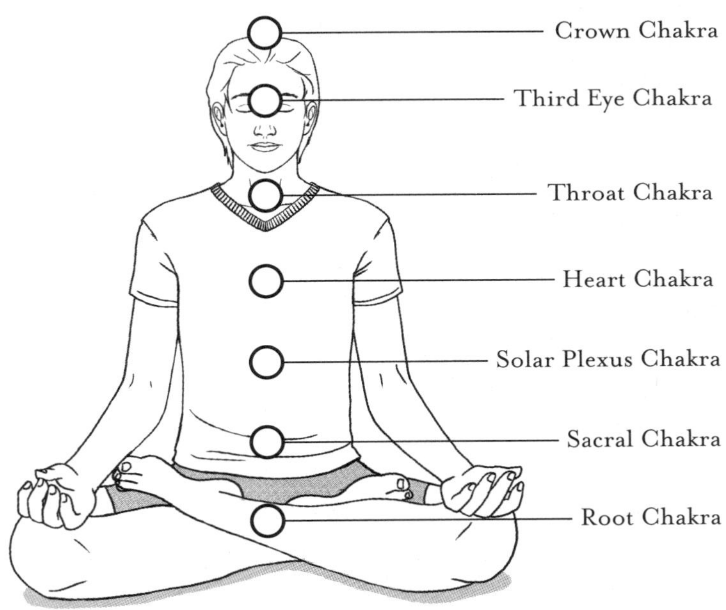

Of those chakras, each corresponds to a color that correlates with the rainbow spectrum of light. This is profoundly symbolic and reflects the understanding of human energy and wellness, which complements this book. I think spirituality and science are intrinsically connected. The rainbow spectrum of light is an energy that is fundamental to how people function and influences us in every aspect of life, from our physical health to emotion to sleep patterns, helping us balance our energy overall by maintaining a healthy state. It is also the reason people are able to see any colors at all. This, too, complements the message of this book, as your intuition communicates to you through light energy that is received by your body.

When the chakra exercises in this book are practiced regularly, they can bring about significant improvements in your emotional and physical well-being. So, whether or not you are familiar with the chakras, I highly encourage you to practice the chakra exercises at the end of each chapter.

A Bit About Me

I've been intuitive for as long as I can remember. My intuition has been a significant part of my life since childhood, even though I didn't have a name for it then. When I say I'm intuitive, that means I use intuition often by allowing my enhanced awareness to help me understand my environment.

I learned there was something more happening in life when I was around six years old. Most of my childhood experiences are fuzzy, but what I am clear about is that as a child, I knew I was more than just my physical body. I had experiences I didn't understand, and I knew they were meaningful in some way. For example, I would know something that the adults around me were not always honest about, which confused me. I mostly ignored those experiences, thinking they were happening inside me and not always knowing that they also connected to the world around me.

While my childhood experiences made me more attuned to intuition, I'm constantly working on understanding, embracing, and learning for as long as I am in this miraculous body I've been given. It wasn't until adulthood that I realized that not everyone experiences life like I do. Getting to that understanding has been a long struggle, and I've studied myself along the way to better understand myself and my experiences. Intuition has shaped my understanding of my life and life in general.

My adult relationship with intuition has been tumultuous, primarily because I am a trauma survivor who repressed my trauma for many years. Dealing with that trauma created a significant barrier to accessing my intuition. As I began to work through my trauma, my intuition guided me to explore a range of curiosities, interests, behaviors, and experiences that ultimately led me to acknowledge that something horrible had happened to me. I then had to confront that realization and live my truth as my crucial first step toward healing.

The more I became aware of, understood, and engaged with my intuition, the more my life expanded. I learned to live more fully rather than just getting by. I credit my intuition with my ability to heal myself, which has deepened my understanding of intuition as a vital self-care tool. This understanding motivates me to share my journey with you.

Believe it or not, life is loving. I know it doesn't always seem that way, but my lived experiences have proven it to me. To date, intuition has been the guiding force behind this realization.

Weaving my experiences as an intuitive and as a trauma survivor has helped me reach a place of self-acceptance that enables me to sustain inner peace. The trauma led me to healing, which took me back to my naturally highly intuitive self. Healing was found by listening to the whole of me, which enabled my life to change drastically. That change has been life-saving, as I was more overwhelmed by the stress from the trauma than I knew. Everything in this book stems from my experience of being an intuitive and a trauma survivor.

Using my intuition brings me joy, much like the joy I experience when enjoying nature, laughing with friends, or expressing love. Engaging with my intuition connects me to the true beauty of life and reveals the beauty within myself. This is where the joy lies for me. In intuition, I experience more of what I'm capable of than I ever imagined possible. Intuition has taught me more about how life intends us to live this majestic, grand experience of being human by discovering more awe in life than was ever taught to me. I hope what you glean from my experience will also be transformative for you and whatever you are dealing with, whether you want to make healthy life changes, pursue personal development, achieve your goals, or heal.

Sunflowers

In my day-to-day life, intuition helps me in numerous ways. It gives me clarity and comfort when I am confused or processing an experience. Recently, a family member visited me during my birthday weekend to take me to lunch. Before his visit, I was perplexed about my interpretation of an emotional growth experience I had been having for a long time with someone I was in a situationship with. I told my intuition to give me a sign to indicate that my processing of the experience was accurate so that I could relax and stop overthinking. I specified that the sign should be a sunflower, and I wanted the sign that day. I was wearing myself out with all my thoughts, but if I were to see a sunflower that day, I would know that all was well.

When my family member arrived, we headed to our lunch spot, which was quite a distance away. Because it was a gorgeous, sunny August day in New York City, we decided to walk. I had never walked to this restaurant, so we took random neighborhood streets. Immediately after passing a street perpendicular to the one we were on, I stopped and turned around to walk up that street. Midway down that street, I found a family of sunflowers growing out of a tree bed. I gasped and inwardly giggled to myself; I got my sign.

My family member and I proceeded to the restaurant, ate, and talked. About two hours later, we took a cab to a favorite park of mine. The cab dropped us off, and we walked the park for about three hours. While leaving, we exited the park at the same place where we entered. Guess what? There were more sunflowers! This time, they were next to the bike lane in a tree bed, directly in front of the entrance to the park. I hadn't even noticed them when we arrived. I was delighted to have that second reminder as we left. My intuition made me pay attention again in case the sign wasn't clear to me the first time.

Guidance via a Reiki Master

Many years prior, in 2012, I "accidentally" learned I'm claircognizant. I had scheduled an appointment with a Reiki Master to have my chakras aligned. On the day of the appointment, when I arrived at her home, she told me she was going to attune me to

Reiki. She had prepared for that, and I followed her lead out of respect for her. We walked from her home to a public park about four blocks away and began studying Reiki. As our time continued, she started praying over me as part of the attunement.

After about four hours or so of study and prayer, a tall man walked up to us and asked what we were doing. I told him I was being attuned to Reiki, and he then asked if I wanted to practice on him. I looked to the Reiki Master for the answer, and she said yes. "The Universe always sends you exactly what you need when you need it."

The man took his shoes off and laid on his back on the blanket in the grass, and I started doing what I was just taught. I started touching the soles of his socked feet, and I began to get concrete information about his wife and daughter. I asked the Reiki Master if I could talk so I could tell him what I was sensing; Reiki is a silent practice, without talking. She said of course, so I did.

The man was feeling guilty about buying an apartment for his daughter, who was his only child and was recently out of rehab. The guilt was twofold, as he felt responsible for her challenges with addiction and about buying her an apartment, as if that act would make up for what he saw as his parental shortcomings. On top of that, his daughter wanted her boyfriend to move in with her.

By the time I made my way up his body to the top of his head, I had a whole story. The man said nothing until it was over and then asked, "How did you know all that? You are exactly right."

I replied, "I have no idea. I have never done that in my life until this very moment."

Clairtangency is spiritual communication that enables me to receive intuitive messages through my sense of touch. (I will share more about other types of clairs in chapter 1.) That experience showed me that it was time I knew more about myself. I express clairtangency when I have spiritual readings with clients to share helpful information about their lives. I touch their bodies, targeting their seven main chakras as my connection to them, which guides my clairtangent readings. Since 2020, I've also been sharing remote readings, touching a teddy bear instead of the person's physical body. There is no difference between in-person readings, when I touch the person's body, and remote readings, when I touch the teddy. During remote readings, I talk to the person on the phone, and the teddy is a conduit for me to attune to their body from a distance. This tells me that my brain understands what is happening too. Using the teddy is my brain's way of helping me understand how I'm able to connect with the person and give them a reading at a distance.

Some of my intuitive proclivities likely come from my family's makeup on my maternal and paternal sides, most notably my maternal great-grandmother, who read palms for a living. My maternal grandmother (her daughter) and grandfather were also highly spiritual; she was an Eastern Star and he was a Freemason. All three of those relatives have passed away, and I pay homage to the Spirit of my ancestors. My ancestors' dedication to mysticism, healing, and service lives in me too. Healers on the paternal side of my family worked more traditionally, including my late dad, who worked in the social work field and practiced hypnotism; my sister, who also worked in the social work field; a cousin who has been forwarding social justice all of his professional life; an aunt who teaches sign language; and another aunt who was the principal of a school inside a prison. We're all of the same ilk.

The natural teacher in me is sharing, and I am thrilled and incredibly grateful to do so. I'll sum up my relationship with my intuition with a sentence from a birthday card that I wrote to myself in 2023: "Dear Me: Thank you for being courageous to be who you are and choosing to live life in spiritual truths."

Let's Begin

Be fully present as you engage in this book and its activities to discover and explore yourself and your capacity to access more of your intuition. Being present with yourself will help you better understand your spiritual being, which is having non-physical experiences. Start by mentally choosing to align your spiritual and physical parts now. You can say to yourself, "I choose to come into harmony with the fullness of who I am and align my spiritual and physical self." That single-sentence affirmation will help your psyche line up too. I'll walk you through the rest.

XO,
Eboni

ONE

Intuition 101

HOW DO YOU CURRENTLY define intuition? Do you think it's woo-woo, not a real thing, a superstition, supernatural, or some paranormal ability only special people possess? Maybe you think intuition is about reading people's thoughts. Or you might think of intuition as a nuisance, something that comes up when it's inconvenient, or something you only listen to sometimes. Intuition is none of these. Nor is it exclusive to women, as many believe due to the popularity of the saying about "women's intuition." If you have any other inaccurate associations with intuition, acknowledge them now so they don't get in the way of all that I have to share in this book.

Intuition is a guide that supports people in co-creating their lives and realities. I break down the word *intuition* as *in*, as in inside of you, and *tuition*, which makes me think of teaching or instruction. So, your intuition is a teaching tool. Intuition teaches you more about who you are and what you are capable of through the intuitive experiences you have.

Intuition is a gift of Spirit, rooted in the non-physical, to help people navigate life toward their desires. It is a natural ability; owning it is entirely up to you, though, *and* if you so choose, you can hone this innate ability to develop more advanced intuitive skills. A helpful start in more clearly defining intuition is to go over the basics with intuition's who, what, when, where, why, and how.

- *Who experiences intuition?* Everyone. Intuition is not a privilege of a few but a shared experience. It's a trait that everyone, from human beings to all other living things, possesses.
- *What exactly is intuition?* At its core, intuition is information with multiple interrelated components connected to self-communication. It is an abstract mode of analyzing data to receive spiritual intelligence. That data is precious new information that can enrich every area of life by supporting you with what you already know.
- *When is intuition happening?* Intuition is not a sporadic event but a constant companion, always there to guide and support you. It can even manifest during mundane activities to make you more aware of your surroundings and innermost desires.
- *Where does intuition come from?* Intuition is an aspect of your Divine Spirit that resides within and connects the inner, spiritual, and non-physical worlds with the outer, human, and physical worlds. Your inner world influences all that happens in your outer world.

- *Why does intuition occur?* Intuition's purpose is to guide you toward happiness and enjoyment by experiencing desires that are part of your soul's growth and expansion and that are necessary for your ongoing understanding of life. Intuition is a supremely powerful force that drives you toward your purpose, no matter how big or small and whether you actively seek that purpose or not. Intuition is so devoted to your well-being that it's inseparably linked to your very existence, providing you with a feeling of security and comfort.
- *How does intuition work?* Intuition presents itself through various forms of information via guidance and messages, ranging from significant, life-changing advice to in-the-moment caution in as many ways as you are capable of noticing. Intuitive information guides you to more of what you desire and helps you make healthy and appropriate choices that will lead you there.

Terms like *sixth sense*, *instinct*, and *premonition* better describe intuition. These are not abstract concepts; they are intimate and personal experiences. Intuition's divine nature connects all of us to the universal Divine Spirit represented by many names: Creator, God, Dios, Mother-Father God, Goddess, Jesus, Allah, Jah, the Universe, Life Force, the Most High, Higher Power, Consciousness, or something else. Intuition is a gift of love from the Divine source, a representation of the ever-present love that you are. The name you connect with this part of yourself is insignificant. As you delve deeper into self-discovery, you will understand more about the source of life, whatever name you choose to call it.

The Inner Relationship

Being inside of you makes intuition close enough for you to notice; however, a lack of self-awareness creates distance from yourself, making intuition seem further away than it is, and your relationship with yourself determines that distance. You must learn to make your way to more intuition by becoming more spiritually aware. For this reason, I like to use the word *access* when discussing intuition. Accessing intuition expands spiritual awareness and is a progression in knowing oneself. That progression teaches you to have a massive, intense love affair with yourself, discovering new ways to enjoy life more. These three elements are intertwined: loving yourself, understanding yourself, and enjoying life more. As you witness your intuition working on your behalf, your relationship with yourself becomes more vibrant. How you relate to yourself dictates your relationship with life. Consequently, as your relationship with yourself changes, so will your experience of life, continually motivating you to deepen your understanding of yourself.

You have to create the space for intuition to present more of itself in order to access more intuition. Creating that space is a wander in personal development and managing all the day-to-day life stuff that positions you to live and express your spiritual and physical nature. It is an expansion of self-expression that involves deepening the ways you prioritize and show up for yourself intimately, in ways that no one else needs to know, so you can fully meet yourself in your present-moment experiences, which requires you to focus on yourself.

Focusing on yourself is a choice, particularly important when you are caught up in a chaotic season of life and experiencing change or uncertainty. Your inner relationship becomes strained when in a state of unease. Instead of responding from a place of ease, upset interferes. During challenging times, people are often pushed further from connecting with themselves, opting to remove attention from where it is needed to soothe themselves with outward influence. On top of that, as early as childhood, most of us are taught to seek wisdom and intelligence from sources in the outer world. When challenges arise, people are encouraged to rely on others for solace and advice and to go to trusted friends, family members, and authority figures to help navigate. Frequently, the need for support is so pressing that we turn to people who don't know (and are not capable of knowing or understanding) our personal struggles. In the digital era, too many of us seek comfort on social media and find support from complete strangers who only vaguely relate to or speak to our specific life experiences.

However, you are your greatest source for navigating your life, and ultimately, listening to your intuition leads you to think and take action for yourself, grounding you in self-awareness and reassurance that no one else can give. In the same way you are sure that when you put your foot down on the ground, the ground will meet it, intuition's presence in you is also assured.

So why go outside yourself when you possess a wealth of wisdom within yourself that is available whenever you need it, 24-7, 365 days a year? My reason was having a lack of trust in myself, and I suspect that may be your reason too. Trusting yourself also means trusting the Divine Spirit. Unfortunately, too many of us don't trust ourselves. Accordingly, you may doubt that you have the most powerful and insightful source of guidance you will ever need: your very own intuition.

Connecting Your Subconscious and Conscious Dots

Your consciousness responds to the messages from your subconscious, and intuition bridges these two states. I prefer the word *subconscious* over *unconscious*, as I associate unconsciousness with the state of being in a coma and subconsciousness with being active yet unaware. Throughout the day, you constantly shift between your conscious and subconscious states, often without realizing it, while processing and storing information from the world around you. This dynamic shift occurs at microcellular levels and within your larger bodily systems. You particularly experience this shift while sleeping and dreaming. It also happens when you are preoccupied and do not pay full attention to an activity. For instance, you could be driving on "autopilot" because you're so familiar with the route, but if someone asked you about a detail of one of the streets you passed, you wouldn't know. This shift can also influence your perceptions, like when a short nap feels as refreshing as a long rest. When you position yourself to realize this connection, the information you gain from connecting these states supersedes the information you receive from language or any other means, as it is much more beneficial for your personal life.

Consciousness, in relation to intuition, is the information you become aware of and pay attention to after being subconsciously guided to receive that information in various ways. Intuition starts in your subconscious and seeks to make information accessible by bringing information into your conscious awareness so that you can benefit from it. The benefits of intuitive information are too many to count and sometimes even keep track of. This section, Connecting Your Subconscious and Conscious Dots, speaks to what I've shared thus far and is super important. As spiritual beings, your non-physical aspect links more to your subconscious state; as humans, your physical aspect links more to your conscious state. The connection between your subconscious and conscious states makes you a spiritual being who is having a human (via physical) experience. You experience life through both subconscious and conscious states and non-physical and physical aspects, as the spiritual part uses the physical part of you to have this earthly experience.

When you are in harmony with yourself, balancing your subconscious (non-physical/spiritual) and conscious (physical/human) selves, you can actualize your true nature. This balance allows you to express your most loving and genuine self, deepening your connection to your humanity. The closer you come to achieving this balance, the more aware you become of all that you are and all you are capable of. This alignment empowers you to experience peace, ease, and even bliss, allowing you to show up more authentically in your life. Moreover, as you bridge the gap between your subconscious and conscious states, you facilitate a connection to a greater aspect of the Divine Spirit on Mother Earth. Take that in.

Intuition is the tool that empowers you to manage, nurture, and grow the reciprocal relationship between your subconscious and conscious states. And like any relationship, the more you give, the more you get; as intuition communicates more, the more you listen and respond. The experiences of your intuition guide you to align with bringing your desires into physical reality. As you become more conscious, you become a more powerful creator in that you are better informed when choosing what you want to manifest. Your intuition can guide you in every life situation, including everyday decisions (like selecting the best route to take or whether to go somewhere) and major life choices related to family, health, finances, and home. Using intuition is meant to be easy. The Divine didn't give us this gift to struggle with it! Instead, it's a tool for growth, a means to understand ourselves and our influence. Having a sense of ease throughout life permits what you want and need to present itself to you in order to experience more happiness and joy in life's grandeur.

Subconscious and Conscious as Dark and Light

Our subconscious self lives in the dark, and our conscious self lives in the light. There has been an overwhelming focus on light in the relationship between dark and light in the collective consciousness. That misplaced attention has contributed to so many of us neglecting our intuition, because intuition originates in the dark.

At this stage in our collective consciousness, when qualifying darkness in the spiritual sense, people automatically think of something undesirable. The dark is just the unknown, and the unknown is associated with many things. Some think of the unknown as secrets, murkiness, or something we don't want to look at because the dark is unclear. However, what is unknown is not undesirable.

Understanding polarity takes great awareness. Opposing energies are complementary. Think of other opposing forces: For example, we would think it's silly to think lowly of motion because of stillness, or vice versa. Dark comes before light and can exist without it. However, light cannot exist without the dark. Therein lies the overarching power of darkness. That power is the power of creation. Once something is in the light, it has already progressed beyond the creation phase. Whatever the creation was, it has already been created and can then only be transformed.

Think of dark and darkness as the beginning. Liken it to the thought before something shows up in your physical life. For example, say you've been tired and thinking about taking a break. That thought is just the beginning of what can then lead to you choosing to go on vacation, identifying a place, selecting a date, and making all other plans before you find yourself frolicking on a snow-topped mountain or browning under the sun.

Light is worthy of all the praise it gets. However, accessing light is not the only goal. If one truly aspires to live a spiritually led life, it's imperative to go into the dark. It's admirable to begin the journey to your true self at all, and focusing on light is a start. But it's not possible to experience only light. If light is all that is happening, authenticity in your experience is lacking. The following simple equations can be referred to as needed when thinking about the dark:

Dark=Unknown=Non-physical=Inner=Spiritual=Subconscious

Light=Information=Physical=Outer=Human=Conscious

Intuition's Tenets

To support you in understanding intuition, let's go over some key principles.

Intuition Is Another Form of Intelligence

I equate the ability to show love with intelligence. We typically think of more intelligent people as people with more information; however, that information doesn't have to come from your brain. The information from intuition comes from the most loving part of you, and your brain is not always loving. So much of what the brain knows comes from its experience of the physical world, and what intuition knows comes from its non-physical and physical experience. For that reason, I've come to think of intuition as being so highly intelligent that it is equal to or even more intelligent than the brain. The brain and intuitive intelligence are similar, though, as both require you to learn and then apply that learning to reap the full benefits. Intuition's intelligence can inform what your brain has forgotten, repressed, and suppressed. Learn to trust your intuition like you trust your brain. The true power in life lives on the non-physical side of life because it shows up before the physical does. The non-physicality of intuition has also experienced what the physical body has not experienced and knows what the physical body does not know. The non-physical part of you is what transitions from the earthly body and continues in ways the body is not capable of.

Intuition Is Like a Muscle

You already use your intuition; you just have to recognize and trust it. Intuition is similar to a muscle in that it will atrophy from lack of use; however, it cannot decline to the point where it ceases to exist. So, no matter how long you've been ignoring your intuition, you can always start exercising and strengthening it, empowering yourself with its guidance.

Intuition Is Available Whenever You Want

Intuition is available as needed. If you are dealing with a difficult situation or person, you can immediately find the calm of your intuition. As a result, you will occupy life's beauty (the pleasing and not-so-pleasing kind) more fully as you learn to hold space for all the ways beauty shows up.

Your Intuition Can Guide You to Any Desire

Desire is many things and can be for love, freedom, transparent decision-making, creativity, insight, or anything else your heart sets its sights on.

Sensory Perception

Receiving guidance from intuition connects to sensory perception, so it naturally relates to energy, emotion, sensation, the five primary senses, and the intuitive clair senses. All living things emit energy, are energy, create energy, have energy, or were created by energy. Your energy primarily connects to your non-physical side and is the life force that keeps you alive through your heartbeat and the functions of your physical body. Life-force energy is a force that powers the sun and enlivens the cosmos. Its non-physicality connects to your spiritual nature and enables you to experience life, including emotion, sensation, your primary five senses, and the intuitive clair senses.

Processing everything as energy helps manage intuition. It enables you to create distance between whatever is happening so that you do not take things so seriously, are more light-hearted, remain calm, and move into your non-physical awareness more quickly. All energies feel distinctly different. In my spiritual work, I've learned to differentiate the feelings of energies of deceased and living people, angelic beings, and cosmic forces. For instance, energies from people who have lived on Mother Earth feel more solid compared to the lighter energies of heavenly beings, which have never inhabited a body. Everyone feels energy, and it is not always a conscious choice; it may be a spontaneous process that occurs naturally. You can tune in to energy in more ways than you know. We have access to different forms of energy: mechanical, sound, light, and chemical. Each form has different purposes:

- Mechanical energy connects to motion.
- Sound energy connects to sound waves.
- Light energy connects to visible light.
- Chemical energy connects to atoms and molecules.

Each form of energy provides neural signals that your brain interprets, allowing you to experience and understand your environment.

Most people are familiar with feeling energy in the context of emotion. You know what emotions are, and you're already feeling energy through emotions. Your intuition will use all the emotions you choose to emote because they are highly present in daily life. Emotions are so profound that they transcend the boundaries of three-dimensional space and time. For instance, when you recall a past event, the associated emotion is rekindled. Sometimes you don't need to consciously remember, as an external trigger like a smell can spontaneously evoke an emotion you associate with.

You also experience sensations, like when you get goosebumps or get a feeling from the hairs on your arms. Those feelings are not emotions. Sensations expand your capacity to feel. For example, when you feel someone staring at you or walking too closely behind you, you feel the presence of that person. Sensations are as integral to the human experience as emotions and can help you learn how your intuition communicates with you. Some of us would interpret the same sensation as excitement while others would experience it as anxiety or discomfort. Sensations connect to how your body responds to your inner and outer worlds; you can feel various sensations, from pleasurable to unpleasurable. A pleasurable sensation could be the feeling you get after a yoga class or a workout, or a tingling sensation anywhere in your body. An example of an unpleasant sensation could be when something feels off or out of position, or an ache anywhere in your body.

The Interconnection of Your Five Primary Senses and the Intuitive Clair Senses

Intuition is connected with the five primary senses (touch, taste, sound, smell, and sight), all ways of receiving information, as your intuition uses the primary senses to have intuitive experiences. The information received from intuition is one reason some people think of intuition as an extension of the five primary senses and call it the "sixth sense."

Your senses surface even when you're not thinking about them, like while you are busy at work or walking down the street. You receive information from your senses more times than you can even count in a day. Your intuition will become equally as present for you.

FIVE PRIMARY SENSES

The five senses (touch, taste, sound, smell, and sight) are the tools used to translate mechanical, sound, light, and chemical energy into neural signals that your brain interprets to help you experience the five senses as follows:

- Touching connects to mechanical energy.
- Hearing connects to sound energy.
- Seeing connects to light energy.
- Smelling and tasting connect to chemical energy.

Each sense is a different way of perceiving different forms of energy from your environment. Your intuition uses these senses because they naturally provide information that helps you experience the world. However, your ability to experience the five senses the way most people do is just one aspect of those senses. You can touch, taste, hear, smell, and see much more than you do at any given moment. For example, some people can smell when they are near water; others cannot. It is that ongoing subconscious communication that tells you what to touch, what to smell, where to look, etc., even when you're just walking down a hallway. Due to the five senses' interrelation with the physical body, intuition requires a level of attention to the self that no one teaches you, and you have to choose to learn to cultivate that level of attention with yourself.

INTUITIVE CLAIR SENSES

Some of the words in this section may be new to you. However, these are words you should know because these are experiences you can have (or already are having) that inform, expand, and guide your life. Everyone experiences clair senses and is more proficient with at least one. Let's start with the three that I think of as the lesser-known clairs, because these words are likely new to you.

Clairtangent means "clear touching" and is the ability to receive information via touch. Typically, clairtangent people also experience clairvoyance and clairsentience simultaneously, because touch positively triggers those other clairs.

Clairgustance means "clear tasting" and is the ability to receive information via taste.

Clairolfactance means "clear smelling" and is the ability to receive information via smell.

The following four clairs are more popular.

Clairvoyant means "clear vision" and is the ability to receive information via visions. Some people see information with their physical eyes, as in seeing someone's aura, and others see information in their mind's eye, as in mental images.

Clairsentient means "clear feeling" and is the ability to receive information through feeling. Many people who identify with the word *empath* also have a strong capacity to be clairsentient, but they may not know how to expand their feelings to get the information.

Claircognizant means "clear knowing" and is the ability to receive information via automatic knowing.

Clairaudient means "clear hearing" and is the ability to receive information through sound. Please note that hearing and sound are two different things, so be reminded that we experience the primary senses more actively, we experience the clair senses more passively. Some people hear these sounds through their physical ears, while others access them through the inner ear, similar to self-talk, hearing your voice in your head, or recalling something you have heard.

The five primary senses align with five of the seven intuitive clair senses. However, clairsentience and claircognizance don't obviously connect to the physical self as the other clair senses do. A general rule to distinguish between your primary senses and your clair senses is that you actively process the information from the primary senses, and the clair senses are passively accessed by you.

The Three Levels of Intuition: Beginner, Intermediate, and Advanced

There are levels to everything. Everyone has equal access to experiencing more intuition when they align with the wisdom of the Divine Source that lives within. You have the choice to engage with your intuition at different levels based on how much you trust yourself to be guided by and receive intuitive information. I've come to understand that there are three levels of intuition: beginner, intermediate, and advanced.

Beginner-Level Intuition

This level is about noticing. At this level, you allow passive guidance, recognizing that something is happening in your communication with yourself. However, you don't know if it is intuition.

Intermediate-Level Intuition

This level is about paying attention to guidance and is a more active experience with intuition. At this level, you know you are being guided in some way and get information; however, you may not be able to understand the information you are receiving.

Advanced-Level Intuition

This level is active. At this level, you consistently understand intuitive information. You recognize and receive guidance, and you use intuition to get information about anything you focus on.

I think of two groups in this category. Group One is made up of people who are intuitive and work as spiritual readers of astrology, numerology, tarot cards, energy, auras, or any number of things to get information. This group includes psychics, shamans, mediums, channelers, and the like. All of these are things I've come to think of as being under the umbrella of intuition, as practitioners are connecting to a bevy of guidance, support, and protection.

Group Two is made up of the most successful creatives of all kinds, business professionals, and gifted athletes, musicians, and entertainers who wow us. They also operate from intuition more than others, and maybe more than they know!

Group One and Group Two are the same kind of people: They get in the flow by letting go of everything extraneous and living totally in the moment. Their commonality is their ability to trust themselves more than most people, and that trust contributes considerably to their success.

Please note that not everyone desires to become an advanced intuitive, and that's okay! Using intuition in countless other ways will serve you well.

• • • • • • • • • • •

Remind yourself that no matter what level of intuition you are accessing, you can always move from level to level depending on how much attention you give yourself. Many people already have consistent, intuitive experiences at the beginner and intermediate levels. However, most people don't know this because they either don't believe in intuition, don't recognize their non-physical presence, or don't recognize intuitive experiences consistently enough to acknowledge that they are real.

An Intermediate-Level Example of Intuition

In 2021, a friend I had met over fifteen years ago kept popping into my head. It was not for any reason, and I noticed it happening more and more often. It started as a few seconds one day, then a few more seconds another day, but it went on for about two to three weeks. This friend and I consistently have communication gaps spanning a year or years, and every time we talk, we meet each other in a deep, loving space no matter how much time has passed since our previous conversation; I don't remember how much time had passed between the conversation I'm referencing here and our previous one. However, I knew this was my signal to call.

When I finally called, we talked for over an hour on the phone, catching up on so many ways life had presented itself to both of us. I casually mentioned that I had unexpectedly written a memoir and told her the spiritual themes my memoir centered on. I then shared that I was seeking a literary agent to represent me. My friend told me that she used to work with a literary agent years ago who she thought would be interested. After I sent my manuscript to the agent, she liked my memoir so much that she agreed to represent me, though she represented mainly self-help books.

The agent then asked me to write a self-help book so she could represent that instead of a memoir. As a result, I wrote this book, although I had no intention of ever writing a spiritual self-help book. You would not be reading this right now if that sequence of events—when my intuition repeatedly told me to call my friend at that time—had not happened.

TWO

Recognize Your Intuitive Nudge

MOST OF US DON'T acknowledge intuition even though everyone uses it. A nudge is the first step in intuitive communication, and it's not just casual contact. It's a polite "Hey" from your intuition, signaling the start of this conversation with yourself. A nudge is your intuition's way of asking you to be more present. It's akin to a gentle knock on the door, asking for entry to open up to yourself to continue your intuitive experience and discover what your inner world wants to share. However, this greeting is quiet, understated, and unassuming while also being direct and unmistakable.

Often, people tend to ignore their intuition by not being present enough to recognize a nudge, not acknowledging any nudge they receive is helpful, or not realizing that a past nudge was highly beneficial. Being present is the key to recognizing your intuitive nudge. This recognition leads to responding, making it a crucial step in your growth journey.

At this level of communication, your task is to identify that your intuition is starting a conversation with you.

Types of Nudges

Nudges use various forms of communication, including sensory perception, feeling, physical and emotional responses, and what you notice in the world. There are two basic types of nudge: non-physical and physical.

Non-Physical Nudges

Your intuitive self can communicate with and without words. This may be via new interests that consistently show up in different places, random conversations, and even overheard conversations. A nudge can also be something you seemingly hear for the first time, such as a particular verse in a song you've listened to a thousand times before, but then you understand the meaning of a certain lyric for the first time in a more meaningful way. You resonate with what has meaning for you, even if you don't yet fully understand the meaning. So, the more you specify what is meaningful to you, the more your intuition can assist.

Sometimes your brain may perceive a non-physical nudge as a "voice." This is because your inner wisdom can be so real to you that it is as if someone spoke right into your ear. When a non-physical nudge acts as a voice, you will "hear" it inside of you as a sound of words or messages, similar to hearing a voice. If the notion of hearing voices is triggering and you have a knee-jerk reaction to that idea, know that the information you receive from your intuition will always be loving. Many people are so estranged from intuition that they don't recognize it as originating from a profoundly caring part of themselves that is communicating what it senses and knows.

Non-physical nudges can be abstract and fleeting. They may appear as any one of the following examples:

- A gut instinct
- An overall feeling in your body
- Fluttering in the center of your chest or anywhere in your body
- A creepy sense that something is off
- An unprovoked, strongly negative reaction to a new individual or situation that you know nothing about
- A positive emotional reaction to a new individual or situation that you know nothing about
- Synchronicity (simultaneous occurrence of seemingly unrelated events)
- Hearing music or any other pattern, such as tapping or any outside noise you hear in your environment
- Smells in the air that you like, dislike, or have a strong response to
- Seemingly random or accidental occurrences that are noteworthy to you
- The feeling of being "in the right place at the right time," or maybe feeling like you shouldn't be there at all

Physical Nudges

Physical nudges manifest in the physical world as three-dimensional experiences you can witness, point to, and photograph. These may or may not be in your body, as nudges also link to the surrounding environment. Physical nudges can happen any time, such as while waiting at a red light or in a reception room at an office. A physical nudge could be a sign you drive by or something you read that elicits a response from you. Here are some examples:

- Words or phrases in a book or on television
- Numbers or symbols that catch your attention
- A "Hansel and Gretel" breadcrumb trail of events that lead you to a desirable outcome
- Goosebumps on your skin or hair on your body standing up

These are common nudges you have likely experienced throughout your life and may not have recognized as intuitive guidance.

However, nudges are not limited to the examples I've shared. Nudges can get your attention through curiosity, creativity, and imagination. The possibilities are endless. Your intuition is so intelligent that nudges are crafted specifically for you based on the likelihood of getting your attention. What gets *your* attention may differ from what gets someone else's. Please note that nudges may be perceived differently by people across cultures and may not have the same interpretations in all contexts due to the collective consciousness of a culture. The key is to recognize and reflect on your personal experiences with nudges.

• • • • • • • • • • • •

The more you acknowledge nudges, the more frequently they will appear. Nudges often employ repetition and patterns in intuition's quest to grab your attention. You might start noticing a phrase, a word, an image, or a number more frequently. This increased frequency indicates your heightened noticing of yourself and the world around you, a key concept in understanding how nudges work. The thing you're noticing either for the first time or repeatedly has always been there; the difference is that your intuition now uses it to communicate with you, making you recognize it more than before.

Nudges can be timely. Whenever you recognize a nudge is the right time to do so. Nudges can carry personal significance and a unique feeling of importance that cuts through distractions in your daily routine, making you pay more attention. For example, you may encounter a particular sequence of numbers multiple times but not think much of it due to being busy. However, the one time it strikes you as meaningful, it may be your intuition saying something like, "Remember when you lived at that street address? Something's happening in your life right now that connects personally with something or someone from back then." Nudges often refer to something more profound than their surface appearance.

No nudge is too slight. All nudges will elicit a shift in energy, feeling, sensory perception, and/or physical or emotional responses. Their subtle nature makes it easy for them to be seemingly insignificant, which is why they are often overlooked even though they are important modes of self-communication. You are nurturing your intuition by learning to appreciate and recognize small nudges in your everyday life.

When to Recognize a Nudge

You will generally recognize a nudge in one of three ways.

1. **In the Moment:** You will recognize a nudge in the moment when you are present enough to know that something is happening; even if you don't know what that something is yet, you notice. For example, you might

feel unusually happy or giddy for no apparent reason. Moments like this indicate that your intuitive self is attempting to communicate something you are not yet conscious of, as intuition exists across space and time.

2. **Reactive:** In hindsight, you will recognize something after a nudge has passed and then attempt to apply it. You might have been too busy with something else to be present enough to connect the dots; only after you've had time to reflect on specific events and think about the outcome will you realize it was your intuition. Another example is when you learn more about something you felt uncomfortable with in the past but ignored. For instance, you may have had a job interview with someone you weren't at ease with and accepted the job offer anyway because you needed the work, only to have consistently unpleasant experiences with that person.
3. **Proactive:** Proactive recognition occurs when you set the intention to receive a nudge. Setting the intention to receive a nudge is done in the same way you would generally set an intention, except you're asking for the nudge. This form of intention setting is beneficial when you don't know what to do about something in your life. Start with small, less consequential choices until you learn to get better with this type of nudge. For example, you could say, "I want my body [or some part of the body] to relax when it is safe for me to proceed with anything." Also, setting an intention is more than just mental; it is primarily energetic, because it calms you and opens you up to receive what you intend. If you're happy, pleasant, and highly

energetic, these nudges will be very effective, and you will receive a response faster than expected. Your mental and emotional states play a crucial role in the effectiveness of these nudges. Particularly if your energy is high or low, indicating you are more or less available to receive more energy.

Each type of recognition is equally useful, depending on your circumstances. An in-the-moment nudge can provide information about a current situation, which could be related to an opportunity or your safety. A reactive nudge, on the other hand, gives you information about something that has already happened; although the event has ended, there will be information about yourself or about how you responded that you can, and likely will, apply later. Proactive nudges enable you to set intentions for a specific concern, then go about your day keeping an eye out for that nudge.

EXERCISE
A Proactive Nudge Practice

Purpose: To practice noticing how your body responds to a nudge. This exercise is also really good for practicing being more present.

Nudges typically occur unintentionally and without you having to do anything. However, you can intentionally provoke a nudge. When you deliberately provoke a nudge, life gets more interesting as you get to explore your inner drive. Let's provoke a nudge to notice what comes up.

1. Start by noticing the overall feeling in your body, and pay attention to how your body is responding.
2. Think of three things you've intended to do but have yet to. These could be anything within the realm of possibility for you, such as contacting a friend or family member or visiting another city or country.
3. Spend only five seconds thinking about each task.
4. As you think about each task, witness your physical and emotional responses. Your body will respond in a way that reflects the emotions associated with each task.
5. Did you notice a stronger physical or emotional response to one task over the others? For example, did your breathing change? Did you sigh, take shorter or longer breaths, experience a shift in mood, or find your mouth watering?
6. Consider why you had a stronger response to that particular task. The response you experienced can provide insight into how you feel about doing that task and why you may have been putting it off.
7. If it's difficult to distinguish a difference between how you respond to those three tasks, choose three different tasks that you know will offer a sharper contrast in your response. For example, recall what you want to do and compare your reaction or response with what you don't want to do. Continue until you notice a difference in your sensory perception, feelings, and/or physical or emotional responses to the three tasks.

How to Recognize a Nudge

In response to an intuitive nudge, you may say something like "I just got goosebumps," or "I felt that," or "This is so weird," or "This series of numbers has been popping up a lot lately." Learn to catch yourself when you say or think something along those lines; it's a sign to tune in and go deeper, opening up to whatever your Spirit is communicating.

When you recognize a nudge, do the following:

1. Be calm and at ease, and focus your attention inward. Your spiritual self is waiting to engage.
2. Pay attention to your breath. Notice the rhythm, how your body moves as you breathe, and hear the sound of your breath. Get into the habit of paying attention to your breath by tuning in to it. Multiple exercises in this book will start with the breath, as focusing on the breath is calming and allows you to release resistance.
3. Mentally repeat *All is well* while taking three slow, deep breaths. As you inhale, close your mouth and count to seven while extending your belly out, then exhale with your mouth open for seven seconds while pulling your belly in, and repeat. The point is to make your breathing deep, slow, and calm. Physical and mental ease grease the pipeline between your physical and non-physical self.
4. Look around your environment for additional clues about what the nudge is communicating. Please don't be discouraged if you don't notice anything out of the ordinary. Intuition begins in the non-physical world, where you cannot touch, taste, hear, smell, or see, yet it is still per-

ceivable. If you take notice now, your intuition may alert you to something before it presents itself in your physical life, like something unsafe but avoidable. For instance, let's say you walked into a room and a feeling nudged you. You may then notice and focus on your environment, perhaps seeing something on the floor that you could slip on. In other words, when a nudge occurs, it may be non-physical via a feeling or sensation, but then you may see or otherwise understand the reason for it in your physical environment (and thank yourself for paying attention before it's too late).

5. Let your brain join in the fun by thinking about what is happening presently. Ask yourself, *What is attempting to communicate with me at this moment?* Asking is significant. When you ask yourself this question, you invite your intuition to share more. Questioning causes expansion, and that expansion can change your life.

REPEAT AFTER ME:
I have a spiritual wisdom that communicates with me often.

Nudge Follow Through

Follow through with a nudge by taking inspired action. Taking inspired action will lead you to new experiences and information that will create more desirable experiences, bringing forth more ideas, inspiration, and possibilities to use in your life. Make the choice to follow through when you notice a nudge. It adds to your history of experiencing intuition and builds belief in your relationship with your inner world.

Know that there are no mistakes when relying on intuition because you are learning more about yourself. Foster an attitude of expectancy and surpass your expectations for happiness. Believe that your desire will come to fruition, even if it seems beyond your current means. This expectation will permeate your subconscious, bolstering your efforts to shape your reality. In the meantime, keep an eye on the flow of your life. Trusting your intuition paves the way for barriers and obstacles to dissolve. When these challenges vanish effortlessly, it's a clear sign that you're in harmony with your intuition.

If you don't follow through with a nudge, you weaken your relationship with your intuition. Instead, build that relationship and cultivate a strong partnership by keeping up your end of the bargain.

Examples of follow-through include the following:

- Taking action on what feels pleasing, even if it doesn't make sense at the moment. Things will become clear later on.
- Treating each experience as if it's your first without comparing it to previous experiences. Not comparing is especially important when dealing with a hurtful experience or people who have hurt you. Treating each situation as new creates space for a fresh, pain-free experience.
- Being open-minded and flexible.
- Allowing the situation to unfold naturally.

Following Through to Arrive at More of You

Recognizing intuition comes with practice. Some people associate practice with boredom. If that is you, replace that association with a new one: Practicing intuition is fun! It breaks routine and dispels boredom. Your non-physical self is never boring. Life is endlessly fascinating, and by nurturing your relationship with your non-physical and physical selves, you will always be following a rainbow to the pot of gold that awaits you at the end.

Following through with a nudge requires you to break from your usual routine. You can practice following through by breaking other routines. What are some of your routines? When was the last time you questioned if those routines were fruitful? Doing anything differently signals to yourself that you want to experience life differently. Try some of the following.

- Take a new route to a familiar place. When you do this, you ask for the possibility of something unexpected to happen. Sometimes, taking a different route to a familiar place may lead a person to a lost item. You may bump into a long-lost friend or read a sign about something new in your community.
- Consistently expand your mental space with new ideas about how to live life. Listen to different kinds of music, watch a television show you thought you'd be disinterested in, go to a cultural event that happens in your city every year that you've never been to, or watch a YouTube video you completely disagree with.
- Minimize upset by being mindful of maintaining a leveled emotional state and letting yourself express the emotions you need to express. Don't hold your emotions in or put

them off. Be emotional as a means of regulating yourself so that you stay in tune with your feelings, which will allow you to feel more sensory perception.

- Maintain a calm nervous system by incorporating meditation. At least thirty minutes of meditation practice each day, either at the start or end of the day, is recommended. Even if you only meditate for five minutes, start somewhere! This doesn't mean you have to begin your day in the lotus position if that's not your thing. Meditation can also occur when you are physically active, whether you are working out, playing basketball, or another activity that you are able to give your full attention to. A great start to meditation is to simply practice sitting still and breathing. Even if you don't reach a meditative state, you will still benefit. If you tried meditation and didn't like it, or if you believe you can't meditate, think of meditation as receiving energy. Feel your way in and around your body to access that energy, and let yourself receive that energy. When that feeling fades, that's your cue to stop, and you can move on to doing something else and meditate again when you want to.

Remind yourself that every day of your life doesn't have to be routine. You can wake up one morning and decide to do things differently, even something as small as reversing the order you wash your face and brush your teeth. Think creatively about breaking your routines, and be sure to notice what is new about you when it happens. By paying close attention to what prompts you to do something differently, you will learn to recognize more of your self-communication. These moments are great lessons in prompting more meaningful inner dialogue.

Here are some little things that can make a big difference.

- Choose to enjoy yourself more, even when doing something you don't want to do. For example, if you have a task at work that will take a lot of time to complete and the thought of doing it causes you extreme discontent, do it in smaller intervals and find a way to enjoy doing it, perhaps by maybe making some kind of game out of it. When you say you are enjoying your life, you are speaking more about how you want to feel emotionally, which is a choice.
- Be less predictable. For example, if you typically initiate contact with a friend, don't. Shift that relationship and notice how it flows when you stop initiating.
- Don't be the first to offer to pay when eating out and the check arrives (if that's your habit). For naturally generous people, be mindful of managing your generosity so it is not taken advantage of.
- Only offer your availability when someone needs a favor that you're up to. If you're not up to it, just say no and let the no please you.
- Wait to answer a question in a text message. Give yourself more time so you are responding and not reacting.

REPEAT AFTER ME:
I can trust myself to give myself what I want and need.

Shoulda, Coulda, Woulda, and Missed Opportunities

Not recognizing your intuition can lead to unwanted experiences, which gives intuition a bad rep. People misunderstand it. We have all experienced a time when we didn't let intuition lead. Perhaps you did that when you knew someone was lying to you, but you didn't have proof, so you proceeded anyway and got burned, or if you didn't want to go to an event but went anyway and had a horrible time. Afterward, you may have reflected and thought, *Why did I do that?*

People may blame intuition when something they didn't want to happen happened, even when they knew beforehand that it wouldn't turn out the way they wanted it to. As confusing as that is, this is how confused some people are about intuition. Recognizing and trusting your intuition is the key to avoiding these situations. It's not just about making better choices; it's about feeling empowered to choose to be different.

A Heavy Left Arm and Shoulder-Pad-Like Shoulders

Years ago, there were countless instances when I either didn't understand or was completely unaware that I was experiencing an intuitive nudge. There was one time when I was standing at the counter in a nursery to pay for a plant. A couple walked in the door on my left, and suddenly, my left arm was so stiff that it felt like dead weight. I knew it was my intuition, but I didn't know what it wanted to communicate. I knew that one or both of the people who had walked in were contributing to my intense discomfort, so much so that I didn't even want to look at them again, and I hurried to leave the nursery immediately after paying. Once in the car, the feeling remained. My left arm was highly uncomfortable and the only place in my body with that feeling. I wanted that feeling to stop, but it didn't; it stayed with me for nearly eight hours, even though I tried to ignore it. By the time that feeling left me, I didn't know what made it go away, if I did anything at all to do so, or if the feeling just left me on its own.

There were other times when knowing what to do escaped me, and walking around with slightly raised shoulders was the norm. I thought my raised shoulders were indicative of typical life stress; however, the source of the stress was a lack of knowledge of how to respond to the information my intuition had attempted to communicate. My body clammed up as if shutting out the noise.

In both of these instances, something inside me connected to something outside me. I was utterly unaware that my strong connection to intuition made me extremely sensitive to feeling, evidenced by my heavy left arm and shoulder-pad-like shoulders. At the time of these experiences, I was in a one-sided relationship with intuition, as I hadn't paid enough attention to that part of myself to understand why those experiences occurred or how they could serve me. I was automatically reactive and didn't know how to respond.

Those experiences taught me to start to pay more attention to my body and the reactions it elicited when my intuition began to make itself known. It happened often, as intuition endeavors for a hopeful exchange. Still, my reply needed to be improved so that communication could be more effective.

You're familiar with other cues your body gives you, like when you're hungry, sleepy, or feeling pleasure or pain. This kind of awareness is like that, except it will show up in different ways and places in your body that you may be more or less aware of. Learn about yourself; get into the habit of paying attention to how you feel and what your body is doing at any given time, especially the places in your body you may ignore.

Self-Love Action: Spend Time Alone by Being Quiet

Many people struggle to find time to be alone due to a busy schedule. However, it's essential to make an effort to spend time alone. Doing so provides an opportunity to listen to your Spirit more clearly. In everyday life, your senses are bombarded with stimuli that can distract you, and being in a quiet space helps you filter through these distractions and connect with your true self. Quiet environments position you to listen to your inner thoughts. Spending time alone enables you to perceive the world differently than when with other people. You then have the benefit of not having to respond to the emotions, moods, energies, needs, and whims of others, instead allowing yourself to respond to you more fully.

Alone time is also valuable for connecting with your heart. It's a time for self-connection. During each moment of alone time, you can focus on feeling rather than thinking, observing rather than reacting. Some problems and issues may even resolve themselves as you become inspired by a new way to address them. Stay quiet, calm, and open-minded, and notice what you become aware of during alone time by trying the following examples.

- Spend alone time every day for one week. This supports your spiritual and mental health as you can choose to only think about what you want. Please do this at a regularly scheduled time, for example, in place of when you watch your favorite five o'clock news or eight o'clock television show. When you habitually dedicate that time to yourself, it can become a regularly scheduled activity. Give yourself this attention for fifteen minutes to an hour; take out a journal and write down the thoughts you want to be thinking, and only those thoughts. Then, reread those thoughts to yourself and save them so you can reread them as necessary.

- Host a silent retreat at home or create a "go into silence" practice. If you live with others, tell them you will only talk for a certain period of time, such as the weekdays or from 6:00 a.m. to 6:00 p.m. Outside the selected time, commit to speaking to no one, listen to nothing, and be with only yourself. A silent retreat is an excellent way to come into harmony with yourself and recognize your habits, patterns, and repetitive thoughts and behaviors that either benefit or hinder your relationship with yourself. You can also sit in silence for a while and keep all of your attention on the silence. That silence may speak to you, but not in words—silence speaks to your heart and your inner wisdom.
- When planning your next vacation, consider the rejuvenating power of a staycation. By staying at home, you can design a nurturing environment to spend quality time with yourself and indulge in activities that bring you joy and relaxation. Remember, your well-being is a priority, even during your leisure time.
- Meditate, meditate, meditate. Meditation is an excellent practice for being alone with yourself, and I like it so much I have to mention it again. Meditation also links the subconscious with the conscious.

- Create opportunities to connect with yourself by turning off your cell phone's ringer and notifications, especially social media notifications.

Some other opportunities for alone time that you can create for yourself include:

- While driving to and from work in your car
- While in the shower or bathtub
- While completing a household chore or task, especially if it's a chore no one else wants to do
- While eating lunch at work
- While walking or biking to a destination

I like these examples because they don't require you to go somewhere specific or make a memorable trip; you can actualize these at any time. Continue practicing spending time alone in any way you can, especially while you are reading this book.

Key Takeaways

- Recognize that a nudge is a type of self-communication.
- Understand that nudges can appear anywhere in your reality.
- Take responsibility for recognizing your nudges and learn how to respond to them effectively.

A nudge is a subtle form of self-communication, serving as a gentle reminder or prompt from within. These nudges manifest in various aspects of daily life, from fleeting thoughts that arise during routine tasks to feelings that guide decisions in significant moments. Recognizing these nudges is essential, as they can provide valuable insight into your true desires and intentions. They may arise in the form of a sudden urge to pursue a passion, a lingering thought that encourages a change in perspective, or even an intuitive feeling that guides our interactions with others. It's important to embrace the responsibility of tuning in to these internal signals. By cultivating awareness of your various forms of nudges, you can learn to respond thoughtfully to the nudges you receive. This response leads to personal growth and enhanced decision-making, ultimately helping you navigate your reality with greater clarity and purpose. Through this process, you can cultivate a deeper connection with yourself and lead a more intentional life.

Reflection: Three Questions

Reflect on what you just read about recognizing your nudges. Write the answers to these questions in your journal, or record yourself answering these questions as a voice memo on your cell phone.

1. Recall three things you became aware of or gave attention to today that you usually overlook. These could be anything, such as the pattern on an elevator wall, if you put your left shoe on before your right, or if the smiley barista at your local coffee shop wasn't there today.
2. Recall at least one moment today when you felt fully present with yourself. Being fully present with yourself means being in the moment, not dwelling on the past or worrying about the future.
3. Did you note to yourself that you were present? If so, how? What were you doing? How did you feel when you were fully present?

The Root Chakra

The root chakra, the first of the seven main chakras, is the key to recognizing your intuitive nudges. It is the foundation for intuition. This chakra is associated with the color red and is located at the base of your spine. It's the anchor that keeps you grounded, ensuring your safety and security in the outer world. Connecting to the root chakra supports you in creating the harmonious balance necessary for clear, intuitive experiences. Before taking any significant action, connecting to the root chakra can enhance feelings of safety, security, and stability. Let your root chakra empower you!

EXERCISE
Connecting with Your Root Chakra

Purpose: To ground you into your energy in order to expand self-support.

Connect with your root chakra the next time you're alone, quiet, comfortable, and in an appropriate place. Maybe you have time to complete this exercise now! It's simple. There is no need for special equipment or expertise, just you and your energy.

1. Set the timer on your cell phone to at least five minutes.
2. Sit quietly, close your eyes, and visualize the color red at the base of your spine; this visualization will connect you to your root chakra. Put all your mental attention on the base of your spine, thinking about it until it is the only thing on your mind and becomes the only place you feel in your body. You could also envision

the color red, or visualize your spine; you may visualize something abstract or picture it as in an anatomy textbook. You can connect to any body part by thinking about it. The thinking sends more energy there and is the connector.

3. Once you've focused on the base of your spine for several minutes, place either of your hands on the base of your spine. Don't be alarmed or surprised if that part of your body is warm because, as you know, where attention goes, energy flows. Feel how warm that part of your body is compared to another part of your body. If you don't feel warmth, that's okay; you will with more practice.
4. Once your timer goes off, reflect on what you just did, and allow yourself to normalize how you can connect with energy.

Trust that this exercise will engage your root chakra and let this part of you know you are thinking of it and loving it up with your touch. You'll feel more physically grounded and supported each time you do this exercise. That support will aid you in connecting with your body to notice intuitive nudges. By engaging the root chakra, you strengthen your foundation for physical security.

THREE

Sharpen Your Inner Awareness

INTUITION'S SUBTLE NATURE MAKES you think it's elusive. Once you recognize a nudge, self-communication expands, and you become more aware of your inner world. Awareness moves you into greater consciousness by acknowledging the nudge and maintaining that presence with yourself to clarify what is happening. The more you do this, the more alert you become in managing this aspect of your relationship with yourself.

Your communication with yourself is nonstop, so you have more than enough opportunities to tune in to your inner world. Most communication with yourself is subtle, similar to nonverbal communication between two people when they are physically in the same space. There is great depth in subtleties, a depth so profound that most of us don't even know how it influences us, which contributes to intuition's mystical nature. Reminder: You are using intuition whether you know it or not, and you are also using intuition whether you want to or not.

Intuition is present before any physical action you take. It's similar to the non-physical instigation of thought that leads to an action, like craving a french fry before eating it. Your intuition guides you in the same way.

Here are various practical presentations of the non-physical already present in your daily life. Increase your awareness of these as part of your relationship with the non-physical.

- **Energy:** You already know.
- **Dreams, Daydreams, Memories, and Time:** All four of these are non-physical.
- **Imagination:** This vast characteristic includes visualizing and picturing scenarios and the images formed in your brain before anything forms in the physical world. It also includes imagining sounds, recalling, and forming ideas in the brain that manifest in the things you create, design, produce, perform, sing, play, paint, sculpt, dance, film, write, and the like.
- **Curiosity:** This characteristic connects to an attitude and a willingness to explore and investigate something new. Expressing your curiosity will help you discover your individuality and uniqueness.
- **Hearing and Sound:** This refers to composed and non-composed sound and includes everything from music to water dripping from the faucet to all of the inner sounds you connect to memories you recall, as all sounds can be guidance.

- **All of the Clair Senses:** Get to know all seven of them, because you are highly gifted in at least one.
- The primary senses of hearing, smelling, and seeing also connect to non-physical attributes, as each involves how your brain processes various signals that you interpret as sound, smell, and sight.
- All forms of mental activity.

Some of the items in this list have supernatural connotations; however, the supernatural also lives inside you and is natural for that reason. You may relate to specific presentations more than others. That is because your intuition is specifically tailored for you and will make itself known in ways that best elicit your response. When you relate to one more than another, your intuition will use that method more. For example, music may improve your mood. Curiosity may excite you. Creativity may encourage you to take action. Dreams may inspire you. It varies for everyone. Please pay attention to what presents itself to you based on what you naturally notice and become aware of rather than looking for it. If you look for it, non-intuitive information can mislead you. As you increase your awareness, you won't have to look—nudges will be literally or metaphorically right in front of you. Being aware also adds a layer of trust in yourself as you witness all the ways your intuition can guide you. Fall back and allow it to do so.

Everyone Is Clair-Something

All of us have spiritual gifts through our intuition; it's just a matter of knowing that you are intuitive and choosing to walk that path and experience life differently. This is one example of how intuition can show up.

At the end of my fifth massage with a woman named Angela, I felt her sensing something specific about me while I lay on the massage table. I asked her if she could pick up energy from her clients. I knew this question was relatable to her because I recognized the spiritual beads she wore around her neck, which represented archetypal energies. Seeing those beads instigated a different conversation with her, and she shared that she indeed picks up energy and that she was writing a book about energy.

I then asked Angela if she ever told her clients what energy she was picking up from them. She said no because no one had asked. I finally asked what she picked up from me that day. She said, "Well, there's someone who wants a cigar."

I had no idea what she might say and was so surprised by her specificity. I said, "Really?" I shared that it must be my dad, who had passed away a few years prior, because he smoked cigars now and then.

"No, this person is older, but it is a man. He's highly protective of you and is with you all the time." Angela went on to say, "You have a picture of him at home."

That was it. Angela left the room, I dressed, we said our goodbyes, and I left.

I went about my day and gave more thought to that conversation again when I was home. I thought it had to be my dad because I have several pictures of him on the wall, but there are pictures of other ancestors on my wall too. I looked at all the pictures closely, and when I got to an image of my maternal great-grandfather Joshua, I saw for the very first time that he was holding a cigar. This image had hung in my home for years, but I had paid no attention to his hands and the cigar he held with his right hand! It completely surprised me.

I then went online and purchased some high-quality cigars to place on a table under his framed image to demonstrate that I received his message from Angela, and as a way of giving thanks, appreciation, and gratitude for my great-grandfather Joshua's presence with me. When you receive spiritual messages, no matter how odd they are, it's best to honor your receipt of those messages.

On my next visit with Angela, I asked her if she was clairtangent. She said no and had never heard that word or known that touch could be a spiritual skill. Angela didn't think of herself as clairtangent even though she had effortlessly given me a clairtangent reading. I then told her I believed the message had come from my great-grandfather and that I bought cigars for him. She was happy to have been of assistance.

Emotions, Moods, and Attitudes

Intuition may use emotions, moods, attitudes, and associated characteristics to communicate with you. These characteristics evoke responses in your emotions, mood, and attitude, all of which are evidence of how you feel. Be a witness to yourself. The stronger your response, the more significant the impact of your intuition's communication. Being more aware of yourself supports you in sustaining witnessing to become more observant of yourself. Observation allows you to separate who you are from what you experience.

Feelings include sensory perception and can also be emotional responses. Emotions are high-intensity feelings, like:

- Anger
- Disgust

- Passion
- Sadness
- Surprise
- Confidence
- Worry

When you are feeling an emotion, express it, and use the opportunity to view yourself separately from it.

Moods are temporary, like:

- Nervous
- Happy
- Joyful
- Peaceful
- Light-hearted
- Loving
- Aggressive
- Impatient

When you are moody, notice it, but don't get caught up in that mood.

Attitudes are how you think about something, someone, a situation, or a circumstance:

- Disinterested
- Friendly
- Snobby
- Reserved
- Respectful
- Tolerant

- Understanding
- Empathetic

When you have an attitude, observe it while asking if it is serving you well.

REPEAT AFTER ME:
I am a witness to myself.

Inner World Influence

Just as your inner world influences your outer world, your outer world influences your inner world. In both worlds, you are influenced by where you focus your attention, making it essential to be mindful of your focus. Whether consciously or subconsciously, your attention is a highly influential force. Think of attention as alignment. Everything you give attention to is a level of alignment, as it contributes to what you allow yourself to be aware of. All forms of entertainment, people, media, and your environment are potential influences for what you create in your reality. Therefore, think twice about what you watch, listen to, read, etc. Even if it's your favorite television show, you are choosing to create and mimic some part of what you see in your own life. You are more powerful than you know, and you are responsible for what you allow yourself to be influenced by.

What you allow can be helpful or hurtful, as influence makes you susceptible to creating realities that include experiences you don't desire. Most people consume a lot of media, which makes it the ultimate influencer. When giving your attention to the media, acknowledge that some of what you choose to watch, focus on, take in, and align with is harmful and purely for entertainment;

remain conscious of that. Ask yourself, *Does this nourish my Spirit, or does it serve some other purpose for me?* You can also use media to align with more of what you want. Consciously choose to find something to learn from it, no matter how small, which will allow you to gain something by giving it active attention instead of passively aligning and enabling potential harm.

If you like the tone of a particular television show and how it depicts empathy, communication, or acceptance, watch that show to be influenced in that way. Shift how you allow yourself to watch your favorite crime show, horror movie, or murder mystery. Shift how you listen to certain types of music that speak demeaning messages. You are acclimating to a new way of being, which may include new forms of entertainment and new choices.

EXERCISE
Create Your Inner World Visualization

Purpose: To create a more complementary inner world environment.

Since intuition uses the body, think of accessing your intuition as a place you go in your body to familiarize yourself with your intuition, in the same way you might be familiar with a physical place you frequently visit.

1. Think of your inner world as an abundant, colorful, beautiful garden, and imagine what that garden looks like to you. Imagine in as much detail as possible. The more detail you add, the more real the visualization becomes. The point is to create imagery that makes your inner world more attractive to you, which will in turn

make your intuition more tangible. Make it fantastical, and include all your favorite things that speak to each of the senses. Use the following prompts to aim high and access the most pleasing responses.

Touch: Think about touch anywhere on your body, from head to toe. It could be a touch you are receiving or giving. For example, imagine you're receiving a foot or scalp massage.

Taste: Most of us eat foods we thoroughly enjoy. Think of your favorites.

Sound: Listen to the natural sounds in your environment for something pleasing. If you don't find anything there, listen to recorded natural sounds like rainfall, the ocean waves, a heartbeat, fire crackling, thunderstorms, the wind, or plants rustling. There are many pleasing natural sounds. Be super curious here.

Smell: Recall the best-smelling scent you've ever smelled. Maybe you can't recall anything, in which case you could go to a garden and smell fresh flowers or visit a perfumery for inspiration. Some people are able to make up a pleasing smell without actually smelling it. Your inner world will respond to that too.

Sight: This physical sense is likely the easiest to imagine, as we have so many examples of this in media. What do you want to look at? How do you respond when you're looking at it?

This place is all about you and is uniquely yours, a world that feels as pleasing as it is comforting and reflects your individuality. Focus on the pleasing responses you get from engaging each physical sense as a part of your inner world.

2. Give your inner world a location in your body with a size, shape, and boundaries, like how the United States has boundaries by state. Your inner world should not take up your entire body; that could be too intense to start, so stick to a location for now. The location of your inner world can take up as much or as little space as you choose. You can give your inner world climate conditions that can change, and you can even add landscape details if you have a preference for one kind over another.
3. The more time you put into creating and familiarizing yourself with your inner world, the easier it will be to go there for solace, regardless of how chaotic your outer world may be. Let this place be where you go when you want to tune in to yourself to make conscious contact with your inner world.

REPEAT AFTER ME:

I'm creating my experiences as I go along,
and I have what I want and need.

Noticing Intuition versus Thought

Intuition and thought can be easily mistaken for each other, which is understandable. Both provide information in subtle ways that you may not always be aware of, and both are non-physical. Both also use some aspects of physicality to communicate. Thoughts use your brain, and intuition uses the whole body. Distinguishing intuition and thought is necessary because they can lead to different outcomes. It's important to consistently remind yourself that intuitive messages do not come from your brain and are not your thoughts; the two are entirely different.

Intuition is perception-based and does not come from thoughts. It will guide you to something you didn't think about that is at least equally (and typically more) beneficial to you than a thought would have been.

- Intuition will draw on the sum of your individual life, even memories you don't remember and have forgotten about, to gather information from the totality of your experience. It keeps track of and identifies all desires created from your lived experiences.
- Intuition will share essential information back to you in an unexpected way that you would not have thought about.
- Intuition will appear as a new idea, a unique approach, or dots you hadn't previously connected; this often happens out of nowhere.
- Intuition will compel you to do something without thought or any apparent reason, understanding, or maybe even a liking. It can steer you toward doing something you initially resisted.
- Intuition is a tool that will challenge and expand your brain's capabilities.

Thoughts are often related to common sense, which comes from lessons learned and conclusions based on those lessons.

- Thoughts have less field of vision, so to speak, and can negate painful experiences by suppressing or repressing them.
- Thoughts can be worrisome or problematic, and they can become bothersome to the extent of self-harm when you worry at length. These thoughts are typically unwanted. I've learned to dismiss unwanted thoughts as they arise by thanking the thought, because I want to have thoughts, and then dismissing the unwanted ones by saying, "Thank you, thought. Goodbye."
- Thoughts can disallow you from receiving new information based on prejudices and biases that can impede access to information.
- Thoughts can talk you out of following your intuition. For example, you may think about the inspiration from your intuition and all the ways it can't happen or is problematic, or all the barriers between you and having what you want.

EXERCISE
Noticing Intuition versus Thought

Purpose: To practice your use of discernment.

You will need forty-five to ninety minutes for this exercise.

1. Before you begin, set the tone for relaxation in your space. Sit in your most comfy seat, get a pillow and place it as needed, dim the lights, play music that relaxes you, and light a candle, palo santo, or incense to get some aromatherapy going. Commit to sitting in this quiet place for at least 45 minutes.

2. Once seated, straighten your spine to ensure proper posture. This will help keep you awake as you relax yourself.
3. Close your mouth and focus on breathing through your nose only. Bring your awareness to the nose hairs in both nostrils and think of engaging them.
4. With your mouth closed, inhale for seven seconds while you push your belly out, and then exhale for seven seconds while you pull your belly in. This ensures fuller breath, which encourages relaxation. Notice your shoulders rising and falling. Your shoulders will rise on the inhale and fall on the exhale.
5. Relax the muscles in your body. Starting from the top of your head to your toes, focus on each area of the body and tell it to relax. You do this by bringing your attention to the area while inhaling and exhaling for seven seconds. Think about the places in your body that are tense and prioritize giving your attention to those places. Mentally repeat, *I find safety and connection with my body.*
6. Notice the thoughts that are grabbing your attention. What else are you thinking about? When you notice you are thinking about anything other than that area in your body, take your thoughts back to your body and think about another spot in the body that is tense.
7. Notice how often repetitive information comes through. Continue to think about your body parts and your breath.

8. Notice if the information you are receiving is desirable. You will know it as such if it causes you to relax, smile, pleasantly sigh, or experience any other response that pleases you. Intuition will feel enjoyable in some place in your body, like when you're tickled or giddy about something.
9. If the information you are receiving is desirable, go further to be sure it is intuition and not simply a pleasant thought. Maintain your awareness to observe if you experience ease in knowing or if you begin to judge or evaluate. Intuition will appear without the need for further inquiry.
10. If the information is undesirable, that immediately tells you it is a thought. Let it go.
11. Do this entire exercise three more times.

This exercise aims to strengthen your self-awareness and deepen your inner relationship with yourself by teaching you one way to communicate with yourself. Becoming more aware sharpens your overall perception by giving more attention to your overall self and the cues and signals happening constantly. At any given time, you may be aware of several things, such as feeling cold or hot, being hungry or thirsty, and listening to a noise in your environment.

As you begin to acknowledge more ways you are aware, you will receive more awareness. Sharpening your awareness also shifts your energy, your ideas, and the experience of what you are perceiving, making awareness highly valuable. Note the following highlights about awareness:

- Awareness is always at your disposal, and you can become more aware whenever you choose.
- Awareness is infinite, as you are an infinite being, and there is no end to what you can become aware of.
- Awareness allows you to receive the information that your intuition is attempting to communicate.
- Awareness is the beginning of truth.

Dear Too Many of Us,

Intuition's non-physical inner nature connects to all other parts of your non-physical inner world. Getting to your truths is one of those parts. Your inner world and your truths align as your truths help you better understand how to navigate what is happening in the outer world. There is integrity in finding your truth versus living the truth. Finding truth instead of living it is subtlety in your perceptions of what you individually experience versus what people collectively think.

Finding your truth comes from how you see the world based on your unique experiences and how you process those experiences. Your life is your own. You can manage your reality and make it what you want. Managing your reality means choosing to be aware. You have all the tools and resources.

Living the truth means creating your daily reality based on your life experiences. Collective truth involves participating in the universal and enduring reality we shape together—for example, the shared genetic makeup of all human beings.

XO,
Eboni

Intuition's Reference

Intuition can only guide you to your desires if you tell yourself the truth. The truth about everything, especially how you feel, is the route to what you want because your truths are intuition's reference for guiding you. For instance, admitting you don't like something someone cooked for you is a small truth that can guide your intuition. As you allow your truths, even the small ones, you enable an opening of more extraordinary love to exist in you. The more you tell yourself the truth, the more loving you are to yourself, the more strongly you allow yourself to be guided by intuition, and the faster your desires will come into being.

If you lie to yourself and tell yourself you are okay or happy with something that's not fulfilling, it is much harder for your intuition to guide you past that barrier you've created for yourself. Intuition cannot lead you to information or action that manifests your desired outcome without your truth.

It's essential to recognize that intuition leads directly and indirectly to experiences that deliver what you desire, as it focuses on what is ultimately most beneficial for you. You may need to have experiences before you can actualize what you desire. However, you will get there, incrementally or indirectly, by way of a detour in life as you address what is untrue for you before your desire actualizes. Clarity and honesty are like truth's cousins and are great sharpening instruments.

Clarity

Here are some examples of experiencing clarity with yourself:

- Let yourself cry. When you feel tears building in your eyes, let the emotions flow.

- Purposefully engage in activities that connect with what you desire.
- Own that your desire is valuable and aligned with your truth.
- Know that having any desire proves your ability to manifest it; otherwise, your desire for it wouldn't exist.
- Believe in your worthiness in all areas of your life.
- Practice putting new ways of being with yourself into your daily life.

Notice that these can be realized in your inner or outer world and are messages communicated to your intuition, messages that confirm you're ready to engage with your intuition more deeply and take inspired action.

Honesty

Being in your truth also requires you to be honest with yourself. Let's be clear about what honesty means: Honesty is having integrity about what you want, and it doesn't matter what it is or why you want it. You own, trust, speak, and follow your truth regardless of what anyone else thinks. This kind of honesty will show up in your thoughts, attitudes, words, deeds, and actions. Understanding and harnessing this is your sovereignty and can empower you in your relationships, your creative endeavors, and your sex life. Here are some examples of experiencing honesty with yourself:

Accept emotional experiences. Acceptance involves a range of emotions, from pleasant to not-so-pleasant. Let yourself jump for joy or weep when those emotions surface. Acceptance allows you to accept the fullness of your emotions and experience them instead of pushing them away. Honor them as experiences, then move on. The point is to acknowledge your emotions honestly, which doesn't mean you have to sit with them forever. Emotions are informative. For example, you may learn that an emotion you've consistently expressed about a particular subject in your life is actually not even true for you anymore because you have outgrown and moved on from feeling a specific emotion about a certain something. Still, your expression of it has been habitual even though it no longer resonates.

Let yourself acknowledge what you desire without feeling guilty about how it will affect someone else. This one is tricky because it can connect to your relationships with other people. You may tend to put other people's desires before your own; you may even tell yourself that being this way is sanctimonious. It is not. What is sanctimonious is following what you desire and owning that by taking the actions to have that desire. Trusting your desires is important because they are always leading you somewhere. A desire is not an endpoint; once you attain any desire, you will still desire something else. Desire expands your relationship with yourself by giving you something new to want to experience in life. That's all a desire is, which is why desire is natural. Once you identify the new experience you want, you must make life changes to align with the experiences of the desire. Let's say you want to get out of debt. There are many routes to that, such as spending less, making lifestyle changes, getting another job, or becoming an entrepreneur to generate your own income. In doing all these things, you also change how you spend your time, what you think about, and what you give your attention to, and you incorporate new ways of managing yourself. Some people may not be happy with the changes you make to align with and create the desire you want because those changes may mean that something changes for them too.

Identify where in your life you are misaligned with your desires. A misaligned desire is one that you are pursuing without fulfillment. Lack of fulfillment is how you'll be able to identify a misaligned desire. Misalignment can also be stressful. Your desires will lift you up, make you feel energized and excited, and allow you to enjoy the alignment needed for attainment. Confront yourself about where you need to tell yourself the truth. Two typical scenarios are pursuing higher education because it is expected and not what *you* want or being in a family business instead of following your passion. The reason something isn't filling you up is because something else that is greater will.

Pursue your desires. As the famous corporate saying goes, "Just do it." Take action toward the progress of what you desire. You often know what to do even if you aren't doing it. Take one small step forward in any way that makes you happy. One step will lead to another, and as each step is an alignment, even if you don't know what the next step is yet, it will reveal itself in time. Taking it one step at a time helps you focus on where you are and raises awareness about that step, which will aid you in the next step. Doing with intention is powerful, as each action you take in life is a form of self-communication and an intellectual, logical affirmation of what you are doing. Taking any action also communicates to the world around you. It is like verbally saying, "I'm here," as you may have done when a teacher called your name during attendance.

Speak your truth as needed, even when it is unpopular or you expect an undesirable outcome. Speaking is affirming to you and the world around you in the same way that doing is. Speaking words has a place; just as some words are vulgar, some are sacred to the point that it is akin to blasphemy to use them out of their proper context. Words create energy to use purposefully, thoughtfully, and intentionally, especially spoken words. Speaking your truth can be super hard. Find encouragement in knowing that speaking is also transformational. It shifts the thing being spoken of along the trajectory from thought to actualization. Get into the habit of saying the hard thing out loud; there is so much learning that happens in the process. For example, speaking to a professional colleague about a perceived difference may lead to the discovery that there is no difference, just a miscommunication; the existing difference may be an opportunity to learn something new or do something different; or the experience may be re-routing you. It's also best to stand your ground if speaking becomes divisive. Whatever the case, speaking your truth will feel like a relief to your inner world once you've done it. Regardless of how someone else receives it, speak your truth for yourself. Be mindful of speaking lovingly; practice saying something difficult that you want to say to someone else by speaking it aloud first, until you can deliver your message to another person with love. Let your Spirit speak to you, then let it speak *for* you.

Recognize the inner work you need to do. Look for instances when any of these points or other inner work require your attention. If these ideas are new or challenging, take a moment to acknowledge *Hmm, I need to work on that.* Recognizing inner work positions you to respond differently and do whatever other work comes along with that. With recognition, your work gets done; without it, it doesn't.

When you show up differently in your life, life shows up differently for you. Appreciate the challenging outer-world experiences that require you to delve deeper into what is going on in your inner world. Appreciation helps you move through things faster.

Fear and Doubt

Some people are fearful of attaining what they most desire. When you notice yourself feeling fear or doubt about something you want to experience, or when you are fearful or doubting of how something will turn out, say to yourself, "I choose to experience [the opposite of the fear or doubt] on every level and dimension of existence and being." As a spiritual and physical being, you are multidimensional. You exist in more places than you have an awareness of, even if that existence is simply in someone else's thoughts. With that being said, if the fear or doubt are minimal and the following feels attainable for you, you can also say to yourself, "Thank you for..." My prayers are like the latter, as prayer for me means giving thanks to the Divine Spirit for everything in my life being exactly as it is. I know that life is constantly changing. You, your life, and your happiness are greater than you can imagine.

Not trusting yourself is rooted in fear—fear of something that has rarely, if ever, actually happened. Do you notice when fear creeps in? The typical pronouncements are easy to identify, but I'm not referring to those. I'm talking about the delicate, precise announcements of fear that are internal, that no one but you knows. It may show up as over-thinking, people-pleasing, or self-doubt.

You may feel fear or doubt when you think about something you want for yourself. Being with and observing yourself as you express fear builds your strength by allowing you to own who you are and how you are showing up in that moment, whatever that looks like. Observing yourself doesn't mean that you diminish any expression of yourself. Instead, it expands awareness of how you feel while being present with the feeling by acknowledging it and choosing what you want to do with that feeling.

EXERCISE
Knowing Fear Is Not Real

Purpose: To support you in dismissing fear.

When fear comes up, try this exercise.

1. Breathe through your nose, inhaling and exhaling for seven seconds each. Once you've found a rhythm, close your eyes and continue to use your breath to center and calm yourself.
2. Then, bring your attention inward and mentally tell yourself, "I'm feeling [whatever you feel now]." You may feel a certain emotion, mood, or attitude based

on something that happened earlier today, last week, or last year. Maybe you are already in a calm space because your breath has soothed you, in which case your awareness is already more present. That, too, is great.

3. Let the feeling linger, and become more aware instead of pushing it away.
4. Next, continue your conversation by mentally repeating, "I am fully aware that I feel [an emotion, mood, or attitude]." State this sentence as many times as you need, honoring each feeling that rises up.
5. Maintain attention to your breathing, and breathe through the feelings you've acknowledged. Sit with and be present with them. Breathing will loosen those feelings and allow them to move on to wherever they need to go.

The next time you become aware that you are feeling fear, stay present with that feeling because it will inform you. Being aware of the feeling of fear will teach you that what was mistaken for fear is something else. The thoughts connected to fear are ultimately not real. You can control how you feel. Ask yourself what your fear is masking. What is the real culprit of the feeling showing itself as fear? Be sure to answer these questions so the next time you feel afraid, you'll be able to experience it differently by addressing the real issue.

Be Your Own Guru

Increasing how frequently experiences lead to a more desirable life starts from the inside and works its way out. Knowing yourself includes knowing the parts that only you can discover. No one knows you better than you. Other people will always contribute to you via what you read, hear, and take away from your experiences with them. However, the more you trust yourself, the more you know what you want to accept or reject from others because of what you know is true for you. Be your own guru. That's what the best gurus say.

REPEAT AFTER ME:
I can trust myself more.

Key Takeaways

- Recognize that nudges first appear in the non-physical realm.
- Cultivate discernment, as it is essential for distinguishing intuition from thought.
- You must tell yourself the truth to be guided toward your desires.

Intuition first reveals itself in the subtle realms beyond the physical. Aligning with your deepest desires requires embracing the truth within. Cultivating discernment is key; it enables you to navigate the delicate balance between intuition and fleeting thoughts, ensuring you follow the quieter voice of your true self.

Reflection: Sensory Experiences

Reflect on what you just read in this chapter. Respond to these prompts in your journal, or record yourself answering these prompts as a voice memo on your cell phone.

1. Document your awareness of at least one sensory experience you had today involving one or more of your five senses: touch, sound, sight, smell, and taste. For example, perhaps you are remembering the sound of your neighbor starting their car, the feeling of something between your teeth, or the sensation of a fuzzy sweater.
2. List five things you can see, four things you can touch, three things you can hear, two things you can smell, and one thing you can taste right now.

Self-Love Action: Practice Learning What Is True for You

Knowing what is true for you requires ongoing navigation throughout life. Truth means different things to each of us and can change over time. For example, one person's truth may be in raising a family, but for another person, it could be running a corporation. Your truths may differ from what your family, religion, and experiences have taught you, and these are areas where you've likely already been asking yourself tough questions. Keep asking. Be loyal to yourself in this way, and know that you are your truth.

The Sacral Chakra

The sacral chakra, associated with the color orange, is located below the navel, around the abdomen or womb. This chakra is the home of your creative and sexual energies and connects to how you engage and express yourself in those areas of your life. Sharpening your inner awareness requires nurturing personal expressions. Like many expressions, creative and sexual energies begin as subtle non-physicality before they become expressed in the outer world. When it comes to creativity, know that this also includes how you individually and collectively create the reality you experience on your own and with others. We are all artists in that way, making all human beings creative.

Creativity and sexuality are integral parts of your connection to the Divine Spirit, as both require subtle surrender to the non-physical parts of yourself in order to connect to and manifest through the physical parts of yourself and your life. Surrender is about feeling safe and letting go by releasing perfectionism and anything related. It embraces self-acceptance, whatever the self is and however the self wants to show up at any given time. You get to determine that. Through surrender, you allow yourself to be more easily influenced by Spirit, becoming open to a plethora of new energies, experiences, and feelings that are waiting to be noticed, which greatly transforms your perception of yourself and life. As much as there is joy in the grandeur and relief of surrender, some forms of surrender can be challenging. Surrender is largely mental and emotional, as it requires detaching from false identifications that connect to negative life experiences. How many times has your intuition told you something, but you still didn't feel the need to follow? It's likely because you were not able to fully surrender to, and feel safe with, your intuitive guidance.

Connecting to the sacral chakra inspires healthy expressions in the creative and sexual areas of life, greatly enhancing intuitive abilities by helping you experience life through your Spirit and understand the true nature of your creative and sexual desires. The sacral chakra lives in the same place as the reproductive organs, reinforcing its connections between creative and sexual expressions of all kinds. Nurturing grounding aids in enlivening these connections and the incredible wealth of potential that these expressions manifest.

Grounding with the Sacral Chakra

A healthy exercise to connect to your sacral chakra is to release more of your sensuality through grounding in how you experience your five senses. There are layers to what you touch, taste, hear, smell, and see. People move so fast that we typically focus only on the most obvious physical outer layer and not the non-physical inner layers that connect to the clair senses. Your non-physical inner world senses and perceives as much as—if not more than—your physical outer world. Let yourself become more aware of how the five senses function in your body to expand how you experience the senses in your everyday life.

Touch/Mechanical Energy: Your body receives stimuli from your inner and outer environments all day. Temperature, weather, food and drink, and cues from other people influence your outer world. You have less awareness of the inner stimuli, such as systems that regulate your brain and neuro responses, hormones, and your immune system. Touch happens when you detect any energy that is being transmitted as a sensation. Become more aware of all the ways you experience touch, and mentally note when touch is happening in any way.

Taste/Chemical Energy: Taste is a chemical response to energy. The taste buds on your tongue detect the molecules in your food and drink and convert those via electrical signals to your brain, which the brain processes as the taste of sweet, sour, etc. Understand taste as interpretation. Taste can be influenced by other associations, like emotion, so note that there is also a psychological aspect to taste.

Sound/Sound Energy: We know how the outer ear works. As a reminder, it operates via sound waves that are converted into electrical signals in your eardrum that the brain then interprets into sound. So, let's look into the fascinating world of the inner ear. This is a crucial component of your sensory system that is primarily responsible for maintaining your balance. Unlike the outer ear, it doesn't "hear" in the traditional sense. Instead, it processes sound across various frequencies and aids in detection and sensing, playing a vital role in your equilibrium. That sensing supports your intuition because your inner ear will sense what your outer ear does not. Remind yourself that you have an inner ear too, and listen for its sensing.

Smell/Chemical Energy: Smell is not just a sense but an acute trigger of memory and emotion. Receptors in your nose interact with molecules that are converted into electrical signals for your brain to process. You can form strong associations between a particular smell and a past experience to the extent that the mere presence of that smell can evoke a response, even when it's not actually there.

Sight/Light Energy: Sight is an ability that uses light energy. The retinas of your eyes detects light waves and converts those into electrical signals that your brain interprets as imagery, allowing you to perceive visual information. That's your natural way of being; as wild as that is, you don't even have to think about it. It's happening as long as your eyes are open.

All of the above connect to complex functions of how your brain and psyche process the multitudes of information you receive through your five senses. By understanding how each one works, you can allow yourself to experience more of your five senses.

Let's practice grounding in the present moment through touch/mechanical energy.

EXERCISE
Connecting with Your Sacral Chakra

Purpose: To nurture grounding.

1. Touch a piece of clothing you're wearing. It can be any piece and with any part of your hand: a single finger, three fingers, or your whole palm. Make contact with your clothing.
2. Focus on the sensations you feel on your hand. Notice the texture and temperature. Is the item of clothing soft, rough, or smooth? Does it feel warm or cool against the skin of your hand? Do you notice any subtle movements in the energy in your hand as the fabric shifts under your touch?
3. Keep noticing what you feel. Your focused attention is grounding you. Know that you can ground through focused awareness at any time.

REPEAT AFTER ME:

I surrender to the totality of my self-expression.

Self-Love Action: Turn Problems into Portals

Use your awareness to prioritize choosing how you want to experience life. When you're experiencing something problematic, challenging, or undesirable, go into it with your intuition. Allow your intuition to guide you to the next step by consciously sitting with that scenario and asking your intuition for specific guidance. Refer to the previous sections in this chapter by being honest with yourself, observing yourself, and expanding your awareness about the problem to help you sort out the issue more clearly.

Gain clarity by identifying the exact problem you are having versus the problem you thought you were having. Your intuition will help you turn that problem into a portal by becoming a more extraordinary vessel for love in your perception of what is happening, which can be shocking and leave you in awe of yourself. Get ready and stay ready for what you receive. Your relationship with this part of yourself is like any other, and you want to nurture it with readiness by doing what you are learning in this book.

FOUR

Encourage Self-Trust

THIS CHAPTER IS ABOUT encouraging self-trust. Too often, people do the opposite and encourage a lack of self-trust. Sharpening your inner awareness encourages self-trust because intuition is fundamentally a self-trust tool. When you speak of using intuition, you're speaking of trust because following your own guidance is a matter of trust: You trust that it won't lead you astray, that it's accurate, and that it is true for you. So, trusting intuition is a matter of trusting yourself. An added benefit of trusting yourself is that when you live in that trust, it is another way of being seen because it forwards more authentic responses from you in all areas of life.

Not trusting yourself enacts self-powerlessness. It happens when you don't apply your guidance and instead act and react based on habit or pattern, making many quick to second-guess themselves in multiple ways that add to a lack of self-trust. For example, let's say someone is constantly unsure if they closed their garage door. On numerous occasions, they've made a U-turn to drive back home to double check, only to see that the garage door is closed, as it was the previous time they made a U-turn. Even though this may be considered "small" in the realm of self-trust, it sends peripheral messaging to your self-communication that you think you are not trustworthy, which creates a flawed premise about yourself. If your intuition gives you the feeling that something important has been overlooked, by all means, check to make sure. However, many of us overlook something once in a while, and as long as it's not something that produces a tragic consequence, there's no need to double check.

Another impactful way you may be encouraging a lack of self-trust is by accepting the opinions of others about you and your life, which is another way of second-guessing. I hinted at this in chapter 1. Yes, some people offer grounded advice that you should heed; however, as well-meaning as the advice-givers and dearly loved people in your life are, *you* always know what is best for you. Other people are incapable of knowing that. You have experiences, feelings, and connections that make your life and how you experience it vastly different from the next person. No matter how much someone else knows about your situation or circumstance, they can't understand fully. They have yet to experience what you have experienced in the way you have experienced it, meaning their advice comes from a limited point of view. Listen to yourself only and leave room to be surprised, as intuition may guide you to do something others may advise against.

EXERCISE
Cultivate an Inspired Gut

Purpose: To stop double-checking and second-guessing.

It's helpful to reduce double-checking and second-guessing when it comes to inconsequential scenarios like turning off a light, taking out the trash, removing laundry from the dryer, or watering your plants. Trust that you did the thing you're tempted to double check, and release the need to double check. You can start by performing this exercise when you notice that you are second-guessing yourself.

1. Bring your awareness inside of you by closing your eyes and focusing on the sound of your breath.
2. Identify a place inside you that brings you comfort. Today, it may be the center of your chest; tomorrow, it could be your belly. The key is to identify where you can go inside yourself that makes you feel comforted. You will know when you have found the place because it will immediately be calming.
3. Go to that place in your body.
4. Affirm that you did the thing you think you didn't do, which will likely be easy because you have gone through those motions many times and know the outcome.
5. Then, go about your day and enjoy that inner demonstration of self-trust you cultivated. Return to this practice whenever second-guessing shows up in your life. It's a great way to encourage self-trust.

Sometimes You Have to Allow Things to Be

Before double-checking, ask yourself the following:

- How many times have I double-checked the same thing?
- Why do I double check that thing and not something else?
- What am I afraid will happen that I want to avoid?
- Why am I predicting an undesirable outcome?
- Where did I get the idea of an undesirable outcome in the first place?
- How many times has that outcome occurred in my life?

To develop more trust in yourself, pick one thing that you tend to double check often and continue this practice for as long as possible until you don't feel the need to double check it again.

Although you may have been "wrong" in the past and will be again, self-trust is about self-messaging, not right or wrong. It's crucial to get in the habit of focusing on the message you send to yourself while doing anything. Begin with the message that you have intuition and let that seep all the way in when these second-guessing, double-checking moments come up for you. Trusting that you have intuition will help you trust yourself in general because using intuition will prove its existence, and you will begin to appreciate how it shows up. Affirm the following to yourself by repeating each statement out loud or in your head:

- Not trusting myself is unnatural.
- I learned, directly or indirectly, how to not trust myself.
- Life is intelligent and has already taught me a wealth of valuable lessons.
- There is always more to learn.

- Trusting myself supports my belief in myself.
- I have everything I need to live the life I want.
- I am grateful.

Right/Wrong

There is no "right" with intuition, and there is also no "wrong," either. Right and wrong are concepts tied to self-identity, perfectionism, social anxiety, cultural norms, etc. What do the words *right* and *wrong* even mean?

As you progress through this process, you will experience inaccuracy. Being inaccurate is not the same as being wrong, and being accurate is not the same as being right. Intuition just is. Is it always accurate? Yes, absolutely. Intuition doesn't have a comprehension of inaccuracy. Think of intuition as wisdom: To be intuitive means to be wise, exerting your other intelligence. *You* may be inaccurate in understanding it, but it is always accurate.

You can also make your inaccuracy work for you. When you're inaccurate, that experience provides more information and tells you that you need to be more aware, helping you focus more on yourself. Instead of thinking of inaccuracy as a personal lack, get excited—it means you're closer to being on track! Be easy on yourself and have compassion. As with any new endeavor, it takes time to develop your gift. Developing your gift will depend on how fervent a student you choose to be of yourself as you learn to inform yourself better. You, too, are a gift to life, and developing your gift will show you that.

As you move through the following steps, you will learn how and why your perceptions may have been inaccurate and how to align more closely with the life path that's for you. And remember, what's for you is a discovery process.

Know that you are on your path, even right now, that everyone's path is different, and that no two people are meant to be on the same path. Every one of us is our own version of genius; you have much to contribute to the whole of humanity from the specific vantage point of your life and how you experience it. If people were too similar in how we lived on our paths, we would miss the opportunity for collective expansion. For instance, a person who has experienced great loss may offer a unique perspective on resilience, while someone who has achieved great success may inspire others with their strategies for growth. Many of us are also at different levels of spiritual maturity, which contributes to why lived experiences vary. They are meant to, even though superficially, many lives incorporate the same elements (families, work, etc.). The dynamics of those paths are where the differences lie. Some of us have lived many lives, and others—well, not so much. This contributes to why each of us responds to life in the ways we do. Whatever is happening in your life is for your journey based on what your soul needs to progress in this lifetime. Life's paths include much more than you know is possible.

Managing your need to be right will help you identify an intuitive response, as you may be hiding an intuitive response behind that need. Many of us invest highly in being right and coming up with the perfect answer and the correct response. It may be a pattern that started early in life if being right garnered praise from parents and authority figures and being wrong brought criticism. Praise pleases us; criticism feels terrible for some, especially while young. Being right is a reaction, not a response, based on thoughtfulness and consideration. Ensuring you are always right is insulting to intuition and menacing to the communicative exchange you cultivate in your relationship with your inner world.

REPEAT AFTER ME:
I release my need to be right.

It's time to be more aware of what's behind your need to be right. Let's check in on how invested you are. Reactions to being right or wrong arise from a defensive place and send yourself the message that you aren't safe, creating an inner environment that is unkind, unloving, and dangerously reaffirms untruths about yourself. Releasing the need to be right will help to overcome various obstacles to intuition, including:

The need to maintain false appearances and pretenses. This speaks to keeping up with what you observe in other people's lives via social media or people in your 3D life. You may be so impressed with what you see and hear that you want to make their lifestyle right for you and follow it for yourself. It's okay to admire someone or something and what they have achieved, but be mindful not to over-associate with what does not naturally come from you, and do not follow a path you did not create.

Uncomfortable experiences rooted in being wrong. Being wrong is a formidable teacher. Learn to like it. It provides even more information than being inaccurate about your intuition. When you are completely wrong about something, it is an intense opportunity to pivot and take a long, hard look at what led you to be wrong. Once you identify that, you will improve multiple parts of life. The wrong can also be an idea you have about yourself and your capabilities.

Outdated beliefs. If you easily believe what you've always believed without question, there's some danger in that. I'm using the word *danger* on purpose so you can become aware of the inner danger you can cause yourself. This kind of danger can cause you to seemingly become stuck in repeating patterns and disallows expanded self-awareness. Life is ever-changing, and you are too, hopefully. Invite yourself to change what you think, what you feel, how you experience yourself, and how you live life. Think of the popular phrase "Change is the only constant." Since we typically don't know what a change will bring, most of us assume change won't be very pleasant, and many avoid it at all costs when, in reality, beauty is what will greet you. There is beauty to be found in the change and expansion of yourself when you allow intuition to guide you to experiences you didn't know were possible.

A lack of authenticity. A lack of authenticity gets in the way of creating more meaningful personal and professional relationships. Being right shows up a lot here. In reality, leading from your Spirit enables more significant success in personal and professional relationships by developing greater purpose, satisfaction, and success. Individually, this is found in the expression of authenticity. Collectively, this is found in the relationships between everyone involved.

Intuition's Traits

Knowing intuition's traits will help you recognize it and know when you are second-guessing or double-checking because of stress or anxiety. Intuition has a clear set of personality-like traits that will help you recognize when you are communicating lovingly with yourself. Intuition's traits will:

Be loving. Intuition's guidance and messages will speak to your heart. If the guidance and communication you receive are not loving, this is not your intuition. Intuition's messages and epiphanies will only be loving. Even when you become aware of a hard truth or acknowledge something as it is, your intuition won't share this in ways that hurt you or make you feel that you have to retaliate.

Be actionable. Intuition will require you to do something. Creating desires includes *doing* along with *being*. Love is a verb and a noun, which means love does something. It's the action generated by the expression of feeling.

Be inspiring. Intuition will excite you as you acknowledge the information presenting itself in your life in numerous ways.

Be effortless. Intuition flows naturally with whatever else you're doing at the time.

Expand your capacity to manage yourself. Intuition is a great teacher. Its inner promptings always lead to personal growth.

Lack doubt. Doubt is not even in your awareness when you walk hand in hand with your intuition.

Be quiet. Intuition never presents itself with fanfare and loud noises. It will be quiet yet confident.

A Specific Note on Our Collective Misguided Bias

Confusion around intuition's traits contributes to collective bias and a lack of trust in ourselves and our intuition. Throughout history, intuition has often been associated exclusively with women. This association is rooted in nurturing traits attributed to intuition, such as surrender, receptivity, empathy, tenderness, patience, generosity, and sensuality. However, a balance of nurturing and assertive traits is necessary to access intuition. Some assertive traits include direction, logic, focus, integrity, stability, independence, and discipline. Achieving this balance signifies a well-rounded individual and is reflected in being *and* doing, as nurturing traits are more closely linked to how you are being and assertive traits are more closely linked to what you are doing. Denying any of these traits can lead to looking for external validation. By embodying these traits, one can tap into one's intuition more effectively, as intuition allows for a greater expression of self and fosters a closer relationship with oneself.

Balancing these traits is a journey of self-awareness and self-acceptance. It may require working on embracing more nurturing or assertive traits. The traits people naturally embrace are often influenced by societal gender norms. For example, some men may need to cultivate healthy surrender, while some women may need to embrace their decisiveness.

For acclimating to nurturing traits, I suggest:

Being more sensual. For example, only eat what delightfully pleases you, not just what is left over in the fridge. There are many things one might consider sensual.

Being more creative. For example, write, paint, cook, bake, design, draw, or play an instrument.

Being in your body more. For example, dance or try exercises like yoga, Tai Chi, Qigong, or Pilates. Exercise helps you feel safe in your body and allows you to feel more, since all feelings come through the body.

Being more expressive. For example, singing and spontaneous outpourings are encouraged.

Being more connected to nature. For example, go to the park or a garden.

For acclimating to assertive traits, I suggest:

Being more assertive. For example, take initiative instead of waiting to be told.

Being more decisive. For example, say no and mean it instead of changing your answer later on. Be firm.

Being more goal-oriented. For example, make a plan and be clear about what you want.

Being more boundaried. For example, don't give everyone your attention just because they want it.

Being more confident. For example, have a positive attitude even when you have to work to find the positivity in something.

Being more independent. For example, go by yourself to any event that interests you.

Being more of a critical thinker. For example, think more for yourself by analyzing your judgments and biases.

Embrace both nurturing and assertive traits if you haven't already. If you have, acknowledge that you are supporting your connection to your nurturing and assertive traits.

EXERCISE
Connecting to Mother Earth

Purpose: To feel a flow.

Connecting to Mother Earth is an effective way of tuning in to nurturing energies by feeling a flow. Do the following:

1. Find a comfortable seated position on the floor. You can also use a chair if that suits you best.
2. Place the hand you write with on the center of your chest. Place the other hand on top. Then, close your eyes.
3. Be calm and at ease, and take your attention inward.
4. Now, take three slow breaths with your mouth closed, inflating the stomach as you inhale and contracting it as you exhale. Continue breathing in this way, expanding and contracting your stomach.
5. Relax your eyebrows, jaw, tongue, and all the muscles in your face. Continue moving down your body to your toes, releasing all tension from the muscles, nerves, and organs. Tension indicates stagnant energy, and feeling tension in your body is your body's signal that you need to release the energy you are holding in that place. Massage is a great way to relieve yourself of the tension in your body. When you release in any way, commit to muscle memory what release feels like in your body so you can ultimately relax at will.

6. In your mind's eye, imagine roots connecting your bum to Mother Earth's center. Imagine that Mother Earth's center is Mother Earth's love.
7. Then, feel the love from the center of your chest flowing to the center of Mother Earth.
8. Next, reverse the feeling to feel the love from the center of Mother Earth coming up into the center of your chest.
9. Feel that up-and-down exchange of love between you and Mother Earth for as long as you want. It may help to synchronize with your breathing. Inhale and pull in the love; exhale and send out the love.
10. Now, repeat the exercise after switching which hand is on top.
11. Finally, give thanks by expressing gratitude for one thing that you experienced today.

Flow

The word *flow* has become popular in the Spiritual But Not Religious community. Flow implies a lack of resistance, and with intuition, resistance is what you want to move past. I would use the word *overcome*, but that word itself implies resistance. By saying "flow," you signal the mind to think more like water flowing past an obstacle; it creates a sense of ease.

Now, look back at the previous exercise and think about the energy flow between your love and Mother Earth's love. Were your thoughts clear? Did you fully immerse in the exercise? Did you feel resistance? Did you feel silly? Did you ask yourself, *Why am I doing this?* You're doing it to recognize the feeling of flow.

You're doing it to be clear and unencumbered. You're doing it to connect with your intuition.

REPEAT AFTER ME:
I am flowing with the Divine Spirit.

Self-Love Action: Making Way for Intuition

Show appreciation for intuition by creating time in your life for more of your intuition to show up. Please do not keep a tight schedule where what you do is entirely dictated by what time you have to do something, be somewhere, or go somewhere. Create gaps throughout your daily schedule so you have opportunities to allow yourself to communicate more with your intuition. Schedule time on your calendar to do nothing, and during these moments, sit down and put your cell phone on Do Not Disturb for a certain amount of time. If your calendar is shared and other people see that, great! Put everyone on notice!

Key Takeaways

- There is no absolute distinction between right and wrong.
- Intuition is inherently loving.
- Staying grounded helps you maintain a connection with your reality.

There is no absolute distinction between right and wrong; rather, your intuitive wisdom, rooted in love, guides the way. By staying grounded, you forge a profound connection with reality, empowering yourself to navigate life's journey with clarity and purpose.

Reflection: The Present of Presence

Following up on the time you created in the previous self-love action, respond to this prompt in your journal, or record yourself answering this prompt as a voice memo on your cell phone.

1. Document the gifts you received from the present of presence. Pick one thing that you experienced when you made way for more intuition. Ask yourself, *What did I do? What did I receive?* Think of creating that space as giving yourself a present and opening it to get the gift. Stay present through the growth that you're experiencing.

The Solar Plexus Chakra

The solar plexus is the chakra located in the space just above your stomach. It is associated with the color yellow and supports your self-esteem, willpower, and how you take personal responsibility. Connecting with your intuition reaches all three of these domains. This chakra is also the one that is most often associated with intuition. One common place intuition shows up is as a gut feeling that some refer to as butterflies in the stomach. Many of us have had that feeling. Use your knowledge of gut feelings to become more aware of when that feeling or something similar shows up in another part of your body. Know that it is your intuition in those places too.

EXERCISE
Connecting with Your Solar Plexus Chakra

Purpose: To better acquaint yourself with the butterfly feeling in your belly.

Intuition is instinctive. It exists naturally and inherently and is the human version of animal instinct that all mammals possess. Maintain awareness that intuition is not limited to the feeling in your stomach but can encompass your whole body from head to toe.

Unfortunately, some people think you can only feel intuition in one area of the body and disregard it when felt elsewhere, or they ignore the feeling completely by moving on to something else. Then, the feeling subsides because the attention from the feeling is removed. However, for this exercise, you'll use intuition to free the butterflies in your belly. Remember, following your intuition takes courage.

1. Find a relaxing seated position. Sitting helps draw attention inward and allows you to be less physically active. When you are pacing or walking, your body is moving a lot, which brings more of your awareness to the body and any number of functions, aches, or pains. So, get comfortable and still.
2. Think of a current situation that is making you uncomfortable, be it physical, mental, or emotional. Prioritize an occurrence that happened today. Maybe you're exhausted and can't sleep, you're experiencing social media burnout, or you're having lots of mood swings. Let yourself think about why.

3. As you think of the situation, notice the accompanying feelings in your stomach and/or anywhere else in your body. What do you notice?
4. Be mentally still with the feeling; do not move on to another thought. Stay with the thought and keep expanding by asking yourself questions about the scenario that you have not asked yourself before. Using the example of social media burnout, you may ask yourself things like, *What is causing me to look at social media so much? What am I looking for? How else can I find what I'm looking for?*
5. When you are ready, ask yourself, *What is my next step in this situation?* Beneath the butterflies is the beginning of your answer.
6. Stay in this trusting place with yourself as you move on with your day.

Exercising Your Spirit

I think of the solar plexus chakra as your Spirit's brain if your Spirit needed to have one. This part of the body is so highly intelligent that almost everyone has had the experience of bodily communication, either via the feeling of butterflies in the stomach or another strong gut feeling. Creating movement helps occupy this space so that those energies are always active.

Any core exercise will do this. Core exercises can be intense, but they do not have to be. If you don't want to do a plank, sit-up, or crunch, any movement that forces you to exert effort will suffice. You could bend over into a forward fold, belly dance, jump on a rebounder, or go for a walk. It does not matter what you do as long as you do it consistently and while intending to connect to this chakra. Think of this as exercise for your Spirit and carve out time for it as you would carve out time for other physical exercise.

FIVE

Respond Lovingly

JUDGMENT DIMINISHES POSSIBILITIES. TRUSTING yourself leads you to respond to yourself lovingly, devoid of self-judgment. Knowing you are love itself may be new to you, making that response more challenging, but since intuition lives on a spectrum of unconditional love, you have to get that. Your learning up to this point in life may have included little to nothing about being love itself or having a built-in guidance system, which is your Divine Spirit, a pronouncement of love from yourself to yourself. You might even feel averse to one of these ideas due to conscious or subconscious messages that you don't deserve love. These societal messages, which are often ingrained from a young age, can be formidable and detrimental to your self-perception. Perhaps you were told as a child that self-love is arrogant. Maybe you've been in relationships (romantic and otherwise) where your needs were consistently overlooked. These experiences can shape your beliefs about yourself, and these beliefs can hinder your ability to access your intuition by keeping you at a distance from yourself.

However, by embarking on a journey of self-discovery, you will learn to love and accept yourself more fully and regain control over your self-perception. Remaining nonjudgmental and having a loving response will lead you to grander revelations about life. The life each of us lives is just a sliver of what is possible in the grand scheme of things. The human part of us only understands life from a limited perspective, which is another reason we are gifted with intuition. Intuition gathers information and widens that sliver of perspective, expanding and changing what we thought we knew.

Making judgments also nullifies transformation, individually and collectively, which is ineffective and risky. It is ineffective in that your goal is to expand, and it is risky in that the individual experiences of each of us contribute to the collective knowledge of all of us. You, too, are a variety of endangered species because there is and will only ever be one of you. Therefore, following your intuition, being who only you can be, and offering what only you can offer are paramount.

REPEAT AFTER ME:
I am the embodiment of love.

Self-Love

Not only do most people not know that they are love in the deepest sense, they also often think that being loving only has to do with how they are with others and not with themselves. Expressing love begins with self-love and has a continuous flow. On their own, the words *self* and *love* are words we're so familiar with that we think we know them well when, really, most of us are still figuring out what each means. Getting to know yourself takes a lifetime, and getting to know love...I mean, love is as highly complex as it is simple. Most of us are stumbling around, attempting to understand how to love someone, so it's no wonder that the concept of self-love can be confusing, as the words *self* and *love* are deeply intertwined.

One of the most impactful forms of self-love is how you treat yourself. What you are doing (your physical self) supports you in getting to the being (your non-physical self). For instance, if you enjoy playing soccer because it brings you a sense of joy, playing soccer is the action that allows you to experience joyfulness. Being joyful, in turn, helps you practice being nonjudgmental in life. When you feel joy, you position yourself to be kinder to yourself, reducing self-judgment or eliminating it altogether. The more significant the number of people willing to be nonjudgmental of life's experiences is, the more harmonious life becomes, as the experiences you judge hold much of the beauty and grandeur of life.

If you think or have been told that loving yourself is selfish, it is not. Typical selfishness is ego-based and is motivated by the brain. Self-love means putting yourself first and is a form of self-care that is motivated by the heart, and anything that comes from the heart is not ego. It's about recognizing that you deserve your own exceptional care, just as you would give to those you love. It can be as simple as setting boundaries, taking time for yourself, or speaking kindly to yourself in your thoughts. You're practicing self-love by giving yourself grace, forgiveness, space, comfort, and a listening ear to your needs. In all situations and at all times, it's important to hold the same level of love for yourself as you do for others. When you love yourself, the choices you make will automatically fill you up, allowing you to more readily provide love to others. Self-love is luxurious that way, and it is a rich, elegant, and indulgent practice. Once you start giving self-love to yourself, you'll begin to believe you are deserving of it and all that you desire. It all starts with prioritizing your needs.

REPEAT AFTER ME:
I am dedicated and committed to myself. I'm putting myself first always, and that is okay.

Here are some small yet mighty suggestions you can incorporate as daily morning practices to begin prioritizing yourself more often:

- Give yourself time to acknowledge you are awake before doing anything or jumping out of bed. Thank yourself for resting.
- Start your day by checking in with how you feel and choosing how you want to feel. Recall the feeling of something healthy and pleasing and how that made you feel, and bring that feeling into your body and present-moment experience as best you can.
- Incorporate some level of pampering. Pampering can be done in the shower, at bedtime, while cooking or doing meal prep, or during a morning routine with products or ingredients that you like the most. If you have the time, take a long bath in the morning and dote on yourself by adding bath salts, milk, fresh herbs, flowers, or essential oils.

- Appreciate physical beauty with color and plants, or use aromatherapy in your home as a constant non-physical pleasantry. Let your physical and non-physical senses be surrounded by beauty.

These examples will introduce new ways of being with yourself. If you find any of these practices challenging, that is even more helpful because you will experience significant benefits from them. Practice one thing at a time, and take your time. Each activity draws you into a deeper connection with yourself, inspiring intuition.

REPEAT AFTER ME:
I love myself. I prioritize myself.
I am only loving.

Repeat this affirmation out loud for about five minutes. Afterward, you may feel lighter and less dense. Feeling less dense means you are connecting more with your inner world because that feeling of density comes from experiences in the outer world. If you don't feel relief, it is because you don't believe the affirmation, which is okay; keep repeating it until you do.

Self-Love Examples to Support Intuition

Numerous examples worldwide demonstrate how to cultivate self-love. The examples I'm about to share specifically focus on accessing more of your intuition and support you in cleaning up the vessel that is your body and refining the divinity within you. These practices not only enhance your self-expression of intimacy but also provide an added bonus by improving your ability to connect intimately with others. By deepening your connection with yourself, including all your strengths and vulnerabilities, you become more adept at connecting with and understanding others.

You may encounter challenges as you navigate the ways of being in this section. If you experience difficulty, prioritize self-care by establishing a routine to focus on taking the best care of yourself. For example, wake up, eat, and go to bed at a specific time as part of a basic routine. Carve out time to do what you need to do and *only* what you need to do. Stick to that routine! Be selfish and say no to things that are not part of your routine. If your schedule permits, align your routine with your natural energy cycle by noting the times of day you are most energetic; align activities that require most of your energy during the times you are most energized to do them. Remember, everything is energy.

If you notice that one of the practices in this section is highly uncomfortable, don't force it. Go slowly and take your time. Whatever way of being you are addressing, know that you don't have to address it now. Just note that you don't like something and ask yourself for guidance and support on why and how to address what you are uncomfortable with. Look out for other responses you have that may indicate you're uncomfortable; many people call these responses "tells." Learn what your tell is. For example, you may divert attention from yourself when you're uncomfortable and go scrolling on social media. Whatever your tell is (and we all have tells), acknowledge your tell as best you can while it's happening.

The following ways of being inspire a more intimate relationship with yourself and are self-love practices.

Checkmate Discomfort

As you do the exercises in this book and expand your awareness overall, you may experience discomfort as you feel new energy, emotions, and sensations. Discomfort is temporary. Feeling uncomfortable when allowing yourself to do something different is okay and natural. Instead of trying to distract yourself, try doing nothing. Doing nothing can help you tap into your inner strength while also allowing yourself the space to recharge. So, don't fiddle with your cell phone, walk around, or get something to eat, drink, or smoke. Instead, sit with the feeling of discomfort. By doing nothing, you are giving yourself the chance to work through what is making you uncomfortable. This allows your mind to process any scary thoughts the uncomfortable feelings bring up.

Doing nothing is also a form of acceptance. When you temporarily accept something uncomfortable, you allow yourself to control it. This kind of control is healthy. In addition to doing nothing, become more present when uncomfortable feelings arise, and don't let those feelings go anywhere else. Imagine your pointer finger on those feelings, holding whatever makes you uncomfortable right in place so you can own the feeling and, eventually, feel yourself taking control. Then, note that the thoughts are exaggerated, unrealistic, and fear-based. As your brain presents these boogeyman-like scenarios, dismiss them one by one by acknowledging their falseness.

Being uncomfortable and comfortable are equally beneficial and beautiful, as both are progressive. That is because both are loving; love is a trajectory always on its way to greater love through its many facets. Where you are on that trajectory will depend on your relationship with yourself. Comfort has apparent value and brings clarity to take inspired action. Being uncomfortable often points to where significant growth can occur and is thus a massive leap toward your desires, making discomfort an offering: It gives you insight into its roots when you sit with it.

As you sit in discomfort, you'll notice that sensations shift in your body, indicating that you're doing the work. Once you learn how to sit through uncomfortable feelings, you can practice sitting in discomfort well beyond accessing your intuition. Make discomfort useful in other areas of your life as you progress through discomfort in those areas.

Honor Acceptance

Accept the experiences you have lived, all of them. Instead of pretending to be happy, diminishing hurtful experiences, and going along to get along, allow yourself to accept the emotional experiences that hurt you and address them as needed. Remember, your intuition knows who you are, even the parts hurt by past experiences. When your intuition guides you to address unaddressed issues, it demonstrates your self-love and healing. Your ability to face any challenge is a testament to the love that you are, paving the way for all the loving guidance from your intuition to be accessed. Know this about honor: When you honor yourself, you honor everyone else involved. Honoring yourself lines you up with your truth, which helps others line up with theirs and ultimately fosters a compassionate and considerate environment.

Honoring yourself means putting yourself first, being selfish, doing what you want, and only doing what feels pleasurable to you, even if others disagree, don't understand, or are confused. Honoring yourself can be tricky because it highlights what needs to change. Change often involves others, and it can be hurtful to others who want that part of their life to remain the same. This often demonstrates where healing work is needed in some area of life. However, the key is to trust the process. Give thanks for the hard stuff, and know that when the hard stuff appears, you are expanding your bandwidth, be it mental, emotional, intellectual, etc. Get into the habit of honoring yourself, especially when experiencing something you don't want to experience.

Give Keen Attention to Your Upsets

Pay attention to how you react when upset, nervous, anxious, and uncomfortable. When you are upset, remember to prioritize your health over momentary comfort. Some things that make you comfortable in the moment can be harmful in the long run, such as unhealthy eating, smoking, or leaning on other vices. Strive for synergy between your comfort and your health.

When you are upset, you may teeter-totter into unhealthy behaviors that occur so often that you rely on them without noticing. These behaviors could be mental, emotional, or psychological and may involve others or happen when you are alone. When these behaviors include others, they can be harmful, potentially involving manipulation. Manipulation can occur in any relationship and often stems from one person feeling unloved, leading them to manipulate others to feel loved, which can manifest in many ways.

By paying attention to when you exhibit unhealthy habits, you can minimize the need to rely on them as a reaction. This introspection into your habits and reactions is a key part of self-awareness. When you notice that you are reacting, you can open up options for yourself and choose to respond instead. Reacting is impulsive, whereas responding is thoughtful.

Welcome Self-Reflection

It is essential to examine your negative behaviors. Behaviors such as being hurtful, untruthful, immature, greedy, or dishonest are consequential signals. They indicate that you are not aligned with your true self. If you notice that you, or someone else, are being downright mean and nasty, know that your true self is only capable of love. Anytime anyone is not loving, they are not being themselves. Reflecting on these behaviors is a valuable reminder to find your way back to your path. Observing negative behaviors in others—either people you know or people in the media—can be helpful. This attention can accompany intention and become a framework for acknowledging your own behaviors.

Self-reflection is an inner act of kindness that welcomes your commitment to your intuition. Reflection is an ongoing process, but certain seasons in life are prime times for looking inward and reflecting on what got you here and now. Any time is ripe for self-reflection, but especially when:

- You have a desire for greater spiritual connection (whatever that means for you).
- You have opportunities to spend more time in nature.
- One of your routines changes.
- You experience change in your professional or social circles.
- Any change happens in your life, such as a new school for your child.
- You are navigating the end of a relationship of any kind.
- It is the winter solstice, because there are shorter days and longer nights, and the moon is a great aid for self-reflection.

Embrace Becoming as Your Inheritance

Your becoming is not just a journey; it's a privilege you've inherited. Like any inheritance, it's a treasure to possess. Changing your self-perception is the key to unlocking this privilege. Many people mistakenly believe they're unworthy of their desires, which creates a subconscious barrier to intuition. But remember, using intuition isn't about gaining something new; it's about tapping into what you already have. Intuition is the answer you've been searching for, and it's always been within you. Accept that you deserve it. But more than that, agree with yourself that this is who you are, and in that agreement, find your power.

Own Transformation Through Curiosity

Curiosity helps you explore intuitive insights. Choose to stay in your flow and on your path by following your curiosity and interest even if no one else in your life is interested or wonders why you are. Explore the new thing, idea, or ideology you heard and are curious about, no matter how weird or odd. Expose yourself to different viewpoints through books, podcasts, or conversations with strangers. For example, reading about someone else's life experiences or listening to a motivational speaker can help you understand your life's challenges and opportunities from a new perspective.

Interest in anything new is also a form of inner guidance. Following your curiosity is a transformational act on your journey of self-discovery. Get into the habit of owning transformation by integrating curiosity into your daily life. The following will help you satisfy your curiosity.

Set intentions. This helps you take control of your life, clarifying what you want. Include goal-setting to boost your confidence in achieving your goals.

Try new things. Embrace the joy of exploration, especially if it is something you previously disliked. You may have changed since the last time you tried something.

Create lists to keep track of new interests. This is a simple yet effective practice that can help you stay organized as you manage your curiosity, as the list can be long.

Research topics of interest to learn more. There is so much information out there! Follow what you relate to.

Take classes and workshops. Learn more about topics you're curious about or have had a years-long interest in. There are classes to learn palm reading, sign language, numerology, astrology, and any hobby-like activity you enjoy or want to start.

Join clubs and groups with like-minded people. This is a great way to meet others who are interested in the same topics and may know more about them than you do.

Volunteer. Choose a meaningful cause that you want to learn more about.

Attend events that fill you up with new information. An event could be a book reading or a spiritual, cultural, intellectual, or artistic talk about a subject you don't know much about.

Stay open-minded. It's important to be receptive to things you've never thought about for yourself, like learning more about your ancestors, mythology, or past-life regressions. This openness can lead to profound insights and personal growth.

Appreciate the Alignment

Think of life's revelations as a progression. Life is constantly aligning and rolling out the red carpet for you. I know it doesn't always seem that way. Let's look at the progression of human development as an example. Alignment takes place from infancy to toddlerhood to early childhood to adolescence to early adulthood to late adulthood and encompasses multifaceted biological, psychological, and social progression. A combination of innate drives and environmental factors influenced this alignment.

Incorporate the understanding of alignment occurring in your life as logic to trust yourself better. No matter what's happening or how it makes you feel, your life is a process of creating harmony. I know that can be hard to read. Trust that when things are hard, the systematic series of events will always lead you to something else, something more, and more of what you desire.

Find the beauty in the pain, and use the pain of whatever happened to your benefit. You can do this by approaching your response as what you *get* to do. Get in the habit of beginning sentences with "I get to" rather than "I have to." The more you notice this, the more surreal your pain seems as you create distance and gain an understanding of its purpose. The more you understand this, the more you can train yourself to manage challenges instead of letting them take over.

Stay Committed

Have compassion and patience for yourself. You will wax and wane as you learn lessons that will make you savvier in your understanding of your intuition. You may need to renew your commitment to this path over and over.

REPEAT AFTER ME:
I am evolving and growing into more of who I am through my life experiences.

• • • • • • • • • • •

The examples is this section connect. Do you recognize the theme? Each highlights some level of being uncomfortable, which is why the list began with checkmating discomfort. Discomfort is highly valuable because it elicits a strong response. When you are uncomfortable, you have the added challenge of being authentic and vulnerable about that. This is because discomfort often strips away our social masks and reveals our true feelings and thoughts. When you're responding to something that pleases you, your authenticity and vulnerability come more readily and easily. Responding authentically to discomfort is more influential for you by more strongly affirming your readiness to be guided in life. Depending on where you currently are in your relationship with yourself, your responses to discomfort may be intense, as each will organically stimulate growth to embrace self-acceptance and the personal transformation that intuition posits.

REPEAT AFTER ME:
I release all reactions not aligned with my true self.

EXERCISE
Feeling Yourself Receive Love

Purpose: To feel the love that you are.

This exercise has three parts. Feeling the love that you emanate will help you feel the love around you. To make sure you are well practiced, there are three versions for you to try.

Humans are walking little love bugs. It's essential for you to know that. Identify with being love more than you identify with anything else about yourself.

Option One

This exercise will teach you how to feel love as-needed when life seems to be telling you otherwise.

1. Raise both arms parallel to the floor, palms facing up. Please make sure your hands are the same height as your shoulders.
2. Then, crisscross your arms over your chest, with each hand resting on the opposite shoulder blade. Feel your fingers touching your back if you can; go as far as your range of motion comfortably allows. Your elbows will make a letter *V* in front of your chest and be on top of each other so that are hugging yourself. This position should feel comforting and secure.
3. While hugging yourself, let yourself lean into yourself. Forgive yourself, give grace to yourself, and cry to yourself. Give to yourself in a way you wish someone else would've and did not. It's even more fulfilling when you can give comfort to yourself.

4. Allow yourself to be in this position with yourself for as long as you'd like before going about your day.
5. Get into the habit of hugging yourself.

Option Two

Here is an alternative exercise.

1. Hug yourself and choose to receive all the love that you are.
2. Repeat "I receive all the love that I am" aloud at least thirty times. If you need to do this in public, repeat mentally as needed. Notice your tone and pace. As you receive more of your feelings and energy, your tone and pace may change, and you will begin to resonate more with what you are telling yourself and become more assertive while you speak this affirmation.
3. Change what you repeat to yourself by making it specific to you and stating what you want to create more of in your life. This exercise is a helpful practice for shifting your relationship with yourself. It sends a loving message of readiness. If you are a prayerful person, say a prayer while hugging yourself. Praying will also help you change your inner conversation to be more loving. Take note of when your inner conversation starts changing.
4. Recall something that made you feel loved, safe, and at ease, and allow the feeling to comfort you. You may choose to bring that feeling into everything you do. It

starts with the practice of calling on that feeling intentionally and as part of a personal ritual. As you connect more with feeling the love that you are, you will be able to call on that feeling at will. The more you practice feeling loved, the easier it is to access your intuition.

Option Three

Here is a third modification.

1. Place the hand you write with on the center of your chest. Then, place your other hand on top.
2. With your mouth closed, inhale deeply through your nose and exhale deeply through your mouth. These should be the longest inhales and exhales you've taken all day, at least seven seconds each. Affirm, "I choose to receive all the love guiding me on my life's path." Receive the feeling that comes with the affirmation.
3. If you'd like, you can also incorporate the affirmation "I receive all the love that I am."
4. Continue breathing to feel the energy of love flowing in and around you.
5. Repeat the affirmation aloud or mentally as often as you need to.

REPEAT AFTER ME:

I am right on time for me.

EXERCISE
Abundance as Spiritual Practice

Purpose: To cultivate the feeling of abundance through singing.

Love is abundant, and experiencing abundance is a spiritual practice. Everyone has the power to tap into this abundance by expressing joy and affirmation through song. Singing will immediately connect you to your inner world and is also an inner celebration of sorts, enabled by the motion of air from your lungs that pushes through your closed vocal folds, causing them to reverberate in the body. That movement resonates through the mouth, nasal cavity, and chest and engages all seven primary chakras.

This exercise will help you focus on feeling the inner motion you create when you sing, from the root chakra at the base of your spine to the crown chakra centered at the top of your head.

1. First, take your shoes and socks off so you are barefoot. Then, sit in a relaxing position with both feet on the floor, or sit directly on the ground. Your bare feet touching the ground will help you acclimate to Mother Earth.
2. Tuck your hips, straighten your spine, and open your chest just enough to make your shoulders upright. Look directly in front of you.
3. Raise both arms parallel to the floor, palms facing up. Spread your fingers out and away from each other. Make sure your hands are the same height as your shoulders.
4. Spread your toes out and place equal weight on your toes and your heels.
5. Close your eyes.

6. Sing "I receive all the love that I am" out loud at least thirty times. You'll find a rhythm as that short phrase becomes a song. Keep singing, and put your back into it. Feel the motion in your body!
7. When you stop, note how good you feel now and how much your mood has improved.

Be intentional by singing when you want to activate and cultivate more positive energy. The next time you are preparing for an important meeting or something you want, sing while you do it.

Love Yourself Up

Make time to love yourself! Loving yourself will help you recognize your value and demonstrate to yourself that you are lovable. Take yourself out on a date. Get dressed up, and feel the fun and excitement of spending time with yourself as if you were spending time with a new romantic interest. While on your date, acknowledge the areas in your life that serve you well.

Use the following as prompts for a great conversation with yourself:

- I'm happiest when…
- I feel safest when…
- I make progress when…
- I'm most confident about…
- I'm most bothered by…
- I am/am not ready to address…
- I feel most hurt by…
- I would like more…in my life.

Self-Love Action: First, Do What *You* Want

Too often, people do things because of obligation instead of preference, and it negates their desires. When you put yourself first, this naturally increases your confidence because you are affirming to yourself that what you want matters.

Before making a choice, take a moment to notice if something noteworthy in your inner or outer world is happening and what priority you are giving it. You may tend to ignore those nuanced moments because they happen so quickly that you think they are unimportant. Now that you're learning to expand your intuition, allow yourself to be more present. Asserting yourself is another way of signaling that you are receptive to your intuition.

Consider the benefits of putting yourself first by recognizing when you need your attention. If you are upset, for example, acknowledge that and actively give to yourself in ways that will support you in feeling less upset, happy even. Instead of reverting to a more passive form of managing that upset (such as indulging in your favorite television show), use the moment to be actively present with yourself. Give yourself the attention you need while acknowledging why you need to do so. Paying active attention to yourself could involve taking a rejuvenating nap or enjoying a soothing shower. Water is communicative, so let the water whirl all over you. You could also savor a warm beverage like tea or coffee. Remember, these actions are not just indulgences but are essential for your well-being. In addition, think about what you want to think about, and only think about that.

An Intuition and Love Story

A first and last name popped into my head while working at home. It was the name of someone I had briefly dated many years ago, and I hadn't thought of him in at least ten years. I noted it, thought it was interesting, recalled our dating experience (which ended in a friendly way), and went on with my day.

That night, the same name woke me entirely out of my sleep. His name was associated with a feeling so good that the novelty of the feeling is what woke me. Again, I noted it, thought it was interesting, then went back to sleep.

The following morning, the name came to me again as my left foot hovered in midair, about to go into the shower. This time, I thought, *Should I reach out to him? What is going on?* Then I said to myself, *I'm not doing that! I don't even know how to reach him.* However, the thought of not reaching out felt so intensely wrong (which is the best way I can describe that feeling) that I didn't get into the shower. I was so torn about what to do that instead, while my right hand pulled the shower curtain back to step in, my left foot descended back onto the bathroom mat.

I walked to my computer and googled his name with a few things I remembered from the last time we were in touch. Luckily, I was able to find his contact information. I emailed him and told him that several people from my past had been coming up for me, and he was one of them. He responded, and we ended up meeting up. I experienced love at second sight. By the look on his face when we saw each other again after so many years, he seemed to have experienced it too.

I had been single for many years prior, doing deep healing to prepare myself to be healthy enough for the kind of love I wanted to experience. Two months before I initially reached out, I had asked the Universe for a romantic experience that could prepare me for a long-term partnership; I knew I wasn't yet ready for what I wanted.

Months went by. Then, another beautiful thing happened between us. While half asleep, with my eyes mostly closed, I got out of bed to use the bathroom. While walking from the bathroom back to bed—a very short distance of about fifteen footsteps—my Spirit told me to pray for him. I checked in and asked myself, *Really, Spirit? Because I want to go to sleep. I don't want to pray; praying will take too much time.* But the message to pray for him was so strong that it felt like I had to. There was no other option, so I stopped being fussy about it and started praying.

I didn't know what to pray for. All was well the last time we were in contact a day or so before, and there was no reason to think anything else. Still, I prayed, and since there wasn't any specific reason, I went into a typical prayer for overall well-being. I started with my usual: *Dear Mother-Father God, thank you for unveiling to me the face of the true spiritual sun, hidden by a disc of golden light, so that I may know the truth and do my full duty as I journey toward thy sacred feet.* That's my go-to prayer for anything; it is inspired by the Kate Bush song "Lily." Next, I asked that my true self be present and that "my family who loves me the most" be present with me. I then asked the same for him and prayed that he feel as much comfort, love, and joy on every level and dimension of existence and being as possible.

I prayed for a while. I don't know the exact time, but it was three-something a.m. when I walked to the bathroom, and when I finished praying and looked at the clock, it was 4:44 a.m. I remember the time because that's the title of one of Jay-Z's albums, and he was a fan. I thought that seeing that time added to the fact that I was connecting with him.

I went back to sleep and woke again around 8:00 a.m. I texted him and asked if he was okay, because my intuition had told me otherwise. I also told him about my prayerful time connecting with him. He replied and stated that someone had robbed him while he was on his way home from a bar that night, and while he was physically okay, it shook him.

Those two experiences taught me a lot about how intuition can show up in love. Nothing like this had ever happened before, and having both of these new experiences be with the same person who had been in my life so long ago was a testament to our souls' connection and love for each other.

We've remained in each other's lives, and he was super special to me for multiple reasons that were revealed throughout the course of our experience. I grew so much with him emotionally and learned to be comfortable being vulnerable and speaking my truths in romantic relationships, which had been difficult for me to do prior. He also was a mirror for me. He showed me who I am in the respect he gave me and the value he saw in me that I didn't see in myself.

Intuition and love are a power couple. Your intuition will only be loving when used in any heartfelt situation. Intuition and love influence each other, amplify each other, and bring out the best the other has to offer. That's what exceptional couples do too.

Key Takeaways

- You must prioritize yourself.
- Having integrity in how you manage your inner world and foster self-love.
- Experiencing greater love from around yourself connects you to the love that already exists within you.

You must put yourself first. Nurturing integrity within your inner world cultivates a profound sense of self-love. As you deepen this love for yourself, you unlock a wellspring of affection that already exists within you, connecting you to an abundant reservoir of inner warmth and compassion.

Reflection: Pray to Yourself

Acknowledging yourself as a spiritual being gives you the liberty to pray to this part of yourself as you would pray to other spiritual beings. Respond to this prompt in your journal, or record yourself answering this prompt as a voice memo on your cell phone.

1. Write a prayer to yourself. Make it all yours by using spiritual words and ideas that speak to you. It doesn't have to be formal or fussy. It should be similar to your natural way of speaking to authentically connect with you. For example, my prayer to myself is "I thank my mind, body, soul, and Spirit on every level and dimension of existence and being."
2. Repeat your prayer mentally and verbally to pray to yourself. Over time, you will memorize it and can use it to reconnect with yourself when you feel disconnected.

The Heart Chakra

The heart chakra, which is the fourth chakra, is powerful because it embodies love. The heart chakra is associated with the color green, is located at the center of your chest, and represents self-love and love in all relationships. It helps you recognize your true identity as love and respond lovingly to yourself. Thus, responding to yourself lovingly connects with the heart chakra.

The heart chakra is also protective, as it soothes emotions and love in general holds protective energy. If you feel unsafe in any situation, imagine how love feels by focusing on your heart chakra. Visualize the color green in the center of your chest, relax your shoulders, take a deep breath, and imagine yourself surrounded by the color green until you feel safe or until the unsafe scenario has passed.

REPEAT AFTER ME:
I am powerful because I am loving.

EXERCISE
Connecting with Your Heart Chakra

Purpose: To learn more ways that you are loving.

The heart chakra immediately commands you to shift your awareness, giving you a wider understanding of what you are experiencing and how you can respond. Connecting to it can shift your perception from one extreme to the next, such as shifting from unwelcome to welcome, or from having no ideas to having many. Imagine how you might show up differently and respond to any scenario when your perception expands. What makes you loving? Sometimes, you have to spell it out for yourself. Think about all the ways you are loving yourself in day-to-day life. Be sure to include those things that no one knows. Include personality traits and characteristics you exhibit that are specific, quirky, and unconventional, as well as perspectives, attitudes, beliefs, and habits. Repeat the following to align with each way of being.

1. Checkmate discomfort. Say, "I recognize my work through emotional discomfort as progress."
2. Honor acceptance. Say, "I honor the presence of the Divine Spirit that lives inside me."
3. Give keen attention to your upsets. Say, "I appreciate opportunities that align with my desires."
4. Welcome self-reflection. Say, "I understand that self-reflection nurtures my growth, and I am open to learning from every experience."
5. Embrace becoming as your inheritance. Say, "I am continually reborn by what has hurt me."
6. Own transformation through curiosity. Say, "I trust life and remain in my flow."
7. Appreciate the alignment. Say, "I embrace and value the process of change."
8. Stay committed. Say, "I am grateful for the opportunities to learn more about myself."
9. Ask your brain to connect with your heart chakra to support you in managing, understanding, and getting to the truths that may be difficult for you to acknowledge if the implications of those truths are something you consider too big, too disruptive, or too shameful. Consider how you can shift the dynamic in your relationship with yourself. What habits do you want to form? What changes do you want to make? In what ways do you want to show yourself love? How do you want to respond to other people? What boundaries do you need to set?

SIX

Listen to Your Body

MANY PEOPLE PERSISTENTLY DISREGARD their body's feeling cues and signals. But, when you respond to cues and signals lovingly, you are honoring your body. The body's design is purposefully intricate for autonomous self-regulation. That autonomy naturally instills a sense of trust, as you know that your body will function on its own. Trusting with confidence starts by listening to the feeling cues and signals your body can communicate through energy, emotions, feelings, and sensations. Feeling is the first form of communication, a language of its own when we choose to listen.

Honor your body for allowing yourself the liberty to feel, because without the body, you would not be aware that you feel anything! Your body's intuitive responses constantly share information via feeling cues and signals. Cues passively convey information, and signals more actively convey information. Both are forms of communication your body uses via pleasurable and unpleasurable energy, emotions, feelings, and sensations. Know that your body has the ability to communicate and display a range of feeling cues and signals to share various messages with you because there are many kinds of energy, emotions, feelings, and sensations, and also note that they are usually interconnected. Understanding how your body communicates feeling cues and signals is crucial as you connect with your intuition because they indicate that you are becoming more aware and that something you desire is manifesting and is on its way to you.

In the realm of sensations, you may feel temperature changes, pressure, tingling, numbness, hunger, thirst, fullness, nausea, etc. Some cues and signals evoke comfort, and others may be uncomfortable. All are strong indicators that help you interpret the world through your physical body. For example, we learned as children that it can hurt to be near something hot, like an oven or a fire. For some reason, though, adults forget to rely on the physical body's intelligence for communication. It's time to start listening again now. Being equally aware of how your body communicates feeling cues and signals will help you learn how to navigate your intuition, and you will be able to consider or reflect on something more deeply by listening to your body. Listening to your body is like a birthing of information that connects to having greater awareness.

Some people only associate the body's communication with aches and soreness, but communication from your physical body doesn't have to hurt. These people are likely ignoring other feeling cues and signals without slowing down to connect with themselves and their bodies, overlooking the valuable information their bodies communicate and missing out on intuitive insights.

You can experience pleasurable and unpleasurable feelings and cues and signals as easily and readily as you can experience comfort and discomfort. Happily understand that all pleasant and unpleasant cues and signals are effortless communication aligning you with your desires. Even when the initial cue or signal is unpleasurable or uncomfortable, take comfort in the fact that you are in tune with your intuition.

Some pleasurable feeling cues and sensations are:

- A sense of lightness in your body
- An airy feeling of movement inside or outside the body
- Lack of stress, worry, or upset
- Relaxed jaw
- Relaxed limbs and muscles
- Relaxed shoulders
- Deep, slow breathing
- A healthy appetite
- Happiness
- Giddiness for no apparent reason
- A general feeling of relief

Feeling cues and signals require you to open up and be more receptive to new information, mentally and emotionally. When you notice pleasant cues and signals happening, you'll want to expand them as much as possible. Expand these feelings by telling your brain you like them, and practice muscle memory with these feelings in your body so you can associate them with whatever is causing them; this will help you better recognize their meanings in the future. For example, expand every time your body signals that it feels pleased, like after a great workout, great sex, a great night's sleep, or a great meal. When you feel euphoria and happiness associated with these things, or for no apparent reason, milk that feeling as much as you can by bringing more and more awareness to how pleased you feel and appreciating that feeling, even thanking yourself for it. Feeling pleased and happy is an indication that you are on the right path.

Conversely, the following cues and signals of discomfort are also ways your intuition will use your body to communicate:

- Tightness in the chest, throat, stomach, hips, jaw, or shoulders
- Raised shoulders
- Uneasy breathing or briefly stopping breathing
- Upset stomach
- Soreness and tenderness anywhere
- Density (which can feel unnatural)

Unpleasant feelings are constrictive, and experiencing them tells your body to slow down and take a break. These cues and signals mean you need to be more proactive by actively releasing tightness and uneasiness that can show up anywhere in the body, and you should pinpoint the source(s) of discomfort. This proactive approach is crucial, as it can prevent discomfort from escalating into aches or pain. Please acknowledge when you're feeling uncomfortable, uneasy, or in pain instead of brushing it off due to societal conditioning, and thank yourself for letting you know.

Unfortunately, many people ignore their body's cues and signals, and they keep doing whatever is causing them discomfort. Or they procrastinate addressing discomfort, and it progresses into aches and pains that can expand into illness or disease. Others have become so used to discomfort that they expect it, not knowing that this anticipation causes and perpetuates more discomfort and may be preventing them from feeling better. It's important to understand your role in perpetuating discomfort through anticipation. Be aware of your automatic responses to feeling cues and signals, including how you think about them, by telling your brain when you are uncomfortable even if you tell no one else. Listening to your body is my most straightforward advice for minimizing discomfort, and it is the simplest form of intuition.

Actively listening to your body yields as much benefit as actively listening to someone speaking. Think of your physical body as its own wise, knowing source, and care for your body like you care for people in your outer world. This is not just a suggestion but a responsibility you owe yourself. This form of self-communication, self-understanding, and self-problem-solving makes you more capable and resourceful in your daily life. This chapter is chock-full of exercises to help you connect with and receive an abundance of beauty from your feeling cues and signals.

EXERCISE
Three Breaths

Purpose: To create energetic spaciousness for yourself, with yourself, and by yourself in your body.

Creating energetic spaciousness has many benefits:

- It alerts you to all the feeling places you can visit in your body.
- It connects to your subconscious mind by uncovering hidden memories and insights stored in the body as well as the associated emotions, moods, and attitudes.

- It is a great way to problem-solve because it allows you to access more information from the dormant wisdom inside you.
- It brings a state of peace to your body.

To begin this exercise, turn on instrumental music and light a candle or something that smells pleasant to you. Then, do the following:

1. Sit down in a relaxing position and be still. I recommend sitting in the sunlight or moonlight to feel more supported; sunlight can help you feel supported in engaging your consciousness, and moonlight can engage your subconsciousness.
2. Close your eyes and relax all the muscles in your body, including your facial muscles.
3. Focus only on your breath by listening to your breathing. Pay attention to how and where you feel your breath in your body.
4. With your mouth closed, take ten-second inhales that push your belly out and raise your shoulders and ten-second exhales that pull your belly in and relax the shoulders. Do this for three inhales and three exhales.
5. If you find yourself thinking about something other than your breathing, bring your thoughts back to your breath and focus on it in more detail. For example, notice the feeling of certain places in your body relaxing as you breathe.
6. Take note of your awareness of your body. Where do you feel greater spaciousness?

EXERCISE
Three Breaths (Extended)

Purpose: To practice being in your body.

This longer version of the Three Breaths exercise is for those of you who are less familiar with stillness and need more time to settle in.

1. Sit down in a relaxing position and be still. I recommend sitting in the sunlight or moonlight to feel more supported; sunlight can help you feel supported in engaging your consciousness, and moonlight can engage your subconsciousness.
2. Close your eyes and relax all the muscles in your body, including your facial muscles.
3. Focus only on your breath by listening to your breathing. Pay attention to how and where you feel your breath in your body.
4. With your mouth closed, take ten-second inhales that push your belly out and raise your shoulders and ten-second exhales that pull your belly in and relax the shoulders. Do this for ten inhales and ten exhales.
5. If you find yourself thinking about something other than your breathing, bring your thoughts back to your breath and focus on it in more detail. For example, notice the feeling of certain places in your body relaxing as you breathe.
6. Mentally repeat to yourself, *I surrender so I can receive.* Repeat this affirmation over and over again. Go into a

meditative state as you repeat it, focusing only on your breath and the affirmation.

7. Imagine yourself receiving and feeling peace, stillness, and joy in your body.
8. Do this anywhere at any time. It's especially useful when you have to do something that requires you to have a positive emotion, mood, or attitude, but you don't have it in the moment.

Feel About It

Many people begin sentences with the phrase "I feel" when they're actually sharing something they're thinking. Be mindful of if and when you do that, and be sure to speak accurately and to what is true for you. Paying more attention to this tendency will help you better separate your feelings from your thoughts and will bring more of your attention to feeling in general. It will also help you recognize and minimize outer-world influences from, say, a television commercial that made you think you want to buy something. Thought processes can easily override feeling processes and lead to something undesirable; it is more helpful to focus on *feeling* what to do.

I believe that feelings are more accurate than thoughts. Feeling is more impactful than thinking when it comes to aligning with your desires, as feeling brings desire into your reality in a more tangible way through the body. Get in the habit of consistently asking yourself how you feel. If you tend to get stuck in your thoughts, ask yourself how you feel about what you're thinking.

Intuition can reach every part of your body and can take up as much or as little space as you allow. Intuition is phenomenal that way. Intuitive awareness is an awareness of something your brain has yet to acknowledge, so you won't always immediately know which of your desires is making its way to you. Just go with it and enjoy the feeling of awareness, knowing you will learn more from it later.

EXERCISE
Familiar Places

Purpose: To practice how differently you feel in various environments: stressful, frequent, and impartial.

A helpful way to begin allowing your intuition to communicate with feelings is to pay more attention to how you feel in different environments. Using the pleasant and unpleasant cues and signals provided earlier in this chapter, ask yourself what your body is telling you when you are in each of the following places:

- Your bedroom, shower, or another room at home where you like to be alone
- Your favorite park, tree, place in your yard, or other outdoor place
- A place of worship
- The spa getting a massage or other sort of pampering
- At a restaurant eating your favorite food
- At the gym working out, dancing, or doing anything that minimizes stress

Some examples of stressful environments include the following:

- At work
- The airport
- The doctor's office
- A family gathering
- Sitting in traffic
- The post office

Begin to notice your body, especially in places you frequent. Are your hips or jaws tight? Are your shoulders raised? Is your breathing easy? You may not notice what your body is telling you in that specific moment. Instead, you may notice it in hindsight when you have something to compare the feeling to. It will be easy to differentiate how your body feels in new places versus places you frequent because your body likely feels different in familiar places and spaces—you just hadn't noticed.

Also, check how you feel in places that you consider impartial to acknowledge if you feel happy, unhappy, or something else while being there, such as:

- Grocery or convenience stores
- Walking on a busy street
- On public transportation
- At the gas station
- The lobby of an apartment building
- A dog park

1. When you're ready, use places you already know feel pleasurable or unpleasurable to spend more time with those feelings. Begin to engage with your inner world

about how you feel at any given moment as you engage with the outer world. See what additional information you can learn from your intuition. Be aware of any judgments you may have about what you feel. Accessing intuition is all about seeking the information in the awareness.

2. Check in with your awareness throughout the day, especially when you know you're dealing with a stressful situation or are about to walk into one. You can check in at any time by asking yourself if you're sitting safely, comfortably, and peacefully with yourself in that moment, and if not, why? Doing this before and during stressful situations will greatly aid you in being present, and you will likely have a significantly more appropriate (and less stressful) response.
3. If some part of your body is uncomfortable, ask yourself why. You may not be experiencing physical pain but the discomfort of an emotion or a build-up of discomfort that shows up via a tight jaw, upper back, and neck, for example. Whether you feel comfortable or uncomfortable, these are helpful feeling cues and signals.
4. Once you receive the intuitive information that inspires a new thought or action, it will ultimately feel pleasing because it comes from your loving Spirit, the innermost part of yourself. I say "ultimately" because intuition's guidance can initially appear as a negative response and be undesirable, unpleasurable, or uncomfortable for various reasons connected to your fear associated with what you desire. For example, it may make you feel nervous. However, there are not any negative consequences

to being guided by intuition. Whatever comes from that guidance will always be for your greatest good, even if it may seem like something else on the surface. Sometimes, what is currently active in your life is outdated and not for your ultimate good, and you are guided to move away; you may not understand why until later.

EXERCISE
How to Feel About It

Purpose: To help you tune in; sense energy, emotions, feelings, and sensations; and feel without touching.

In each of the following two parts, the key is to acknowledge the non-physical spaces between physical spaces. This is how you develop a more profound sense of feeling what is non-physical. Whether you feel comfortable or uncomfortable feelings, let yourself become fully aware of them instead of shying away.

Part One

You can do this exercise anywhere and at any time. You can also do it at various intensity levels, depending on whether you are alone or in the company of others.

1. Stand or sit, placing both feet on the floor. Become aware of the ground beneath you.
2. With your mouth closed, take several long, deep breaths and flex all ten toes.
3. Turn both palms face up.

4. Straighten your fingers without tension so they are relaxed and slightly bent.
5. Straighten your spine, relax your shoulders, slightly tuck your chin, and sit or stand upright.
6. Mentally acknowledge if you feel more pleasant or unpleasant feelings or sensations. Is there any place in your body that feels comfortable or uncomfortable? That feeling may be in a specific place, or it may be felt throughout your body.
7. Now, do something fast-moving, like flapping your arms, jumping up and down, or doing a few squats to be energized. If any part of your body feels uncomfortable, it means the energy in that place isn't flowing well and is likely stagnant, so moving around is helpful.
8. After moving around, it may be beneficial to do this exercise again to notice the difference movement makes in your ability to feel when your energy is flowing better.

You're constantly receiving feeling cues and signals. However, many of us feel these feelings so often that we don't even know we're feeling them. Some people think they only experience feeling when a feeling is so extreme that it overwhelms them and makes them notice, but there is so much life in the non-extreme feelings.

You can get into the habit of noticing your feelings just as easily as noticing your thoughts. In the next part, you're going to monitor your feelings. You are already more aware than you acknowledge, but start by playing around if this is a new idea for you. Feel the sun on your arms or your face. Feel the breeze blow across your scalp or cheeks. Feel when hunger is in your belly, spice is on your tongue, and cold is in your nose, like when you have a cold rush from eating ice cream. Practicing what you feel broadens your knowledge and strengthens your belief in the existence of your intuition. Most importantly, this practice is a continuous reminder of all the ways you can feel whenever you need reminding.

Part Two

Practice the following exercise with a friend or family member. Be mindful of who you choose; pick someone who is open to feeling energy. Then, do this exercise privately, just the two of you. The more intimate your relationship with the other person, the better, because there will be a greater comfort level between you two.

1. Hold the palm of your hand about two inches away from the palm of your loved one's hand. What do you feel?
2. Hold the palm of your hand two inches away from your loved one's stomach, near their solar plexus chakra. What do you feel?
3. Hold the palm of your hand about two inches away from the center of your loved one's chest. What do you feel?
4. Sit upright in a comfortable position in front of your loved one and focus your mind on feeling the center of their chest. What do you feel?
5. Sit close to each other without touching. What do you feel?

6. Stand close to each other without touching. What do you feel?
7. Lie on your back. Place the heels of your feet on the floor with your toes pointing toward the ceiling. Ask your loved one to place their feet two inches away from your feet, also with their toes pointed upward. Focus on the feelings between the bottoms of your feet and theirs.
8. Ask your loved one where they feel discomfort in their body, then hold your hand about two inches away from that place. Do you feel their presence? Do you feel their discomfort?

In this exercise, you felt without touching. At first, you may not have felt much of anything because you are so used to feeling by touching, but with practice, you will learn to sense and feel what's present but unseen without touching it.

Everyone's non-physical presence feels different, and all living things have a non-physical presence. You can practice with any person, your pet, or, as you progress, any living thing, including trees and even raw fruits and vegetables. Make it fun! You'll discover how much more colorful the feeling world is. Remember, the more you get used to these yummy feelings that are always accessible to you, the more you can feel them at any time, not just when you're doing the exercises in this book. Please get in the habit of feeling how pleasing life can be by recognizing more and more that these feelings are real and exist whenever you want to access them.

Look around you now and focus on the "empty" spaces instead of the objects, people, and other physical items. What appears to be empty space is not empty at all—it is brimming with energy.

Tinglin' Toes and Sink Bowls

I'm right-handed. Every now and then, these strong inklings come over me and I feel called to do everything with my left hand, so I do. I'll pick up drinking glasses, open doors, brush my teeth, sauté veggies in a pan, and try writing and painting with my left hand. My left-handed activities are sloppy, so I don't go on like that for long, even though it is particularly gratifying because it feels like I'm coming into balance. Leading with my left hand is expressing some part of myself that needs balance. When this happens, it makes me think of ambidextrous people and their right- and left-brain functioning. I'm amazed by that ability. Ambidextrous people must feel balanced in a way that other people do not.

The other day, this left-handed thing started happening again very casually. Usually, I'm aware of it, and when it shows up, I purposefully lead left. This time, it showed up before I was aware. While sitting at my computer, I crossed my left ankle over my right. I didn't cross my ankle for any reason; I just moved in my chair. Then, all the toes on both feet immediately started tingling, and I realized that my left-leading thing was happening. That energy flow went from my left ankle to the right and up my body to the top of my head. It felt like an energetic flutter, best described as the airy movement created by a small bird's flapping wings.

I don't know if I've ever felt my energy like that before, and I often pay attention to the non-physical movement flowing through my body. If you practice yoga, think about the feeling that comes over you at the end of a yoga practice when you're in savasana pose or, if you do not practice yoga, the feeling after you exercise. It was similar to those feelings, but neither of those things had just happened; that feeling of energy flow came over me on its own. It was so yummy that I got excited about it, and my heartbeat sped up. I noted it, took my focus away from the computer screen, and instead focused inward to feel as much as possible while I enjoyed that flow for about twenty minutes. Even though I had planned to get up and do something else, I didn't.

The physical body is a maze for energy, with infinite routes for energy to take and endless ways for energy to move through you. Give this a try in your own way. Cross the hand or foot that is less dominant for you, lie on the side you don't usually lie on, or lead with your nondominant hand. Position your body in atypical ways, and please ensure you are comfortable doing this. Let your body shift its energy in the process. These are simple practices that you can do to expand your awareness of yourself and feel more of what you've never felt before. Notice how you feel when you do it.

My energy was shifting because so many changes were happening inside of me. I understand my awareness of these shifts in my energy as subtle confirmation of change and that I'm allowing myself to have different experiences that come along with shifting energy. All changes take place energetically before they appear in three-dimensional reality. Another way this shift showed itself to me that same day was when my bathroom basin broke. A perfume bottle slipped from my hand and fell into the bathroom sink; part of the bottle broke while also breaking the bowl. In my life, breaking things happens about as often as the left-hand leading thing does. I'm not superstitious and don't connect broken things to undesirable happenings. Actually, I think of it as physics. The energy of the falling perfume bottle was converted into kinetic energy while in motion and then shattered, transforming it into another form of energy. That's a good way to sum up what's happening when our energy shifts too.

EXERCISE
Feeling Yourself

Purpose: To practice feeling in and around your body.

Developing a stronger awareness of feeling yourself helps you feel more of what is outside of you. It expands your ability to feel the non-physical presence around you, be it another person's energy, emotions, or anything else you can feel from other living things. Do the following:

1. Sit cross-legged on the floor with one ankle on top of the other. If your ankles don't meet, that's okay; cross your legs as comfortably as you can.
2. Close your eyes, breathe, and feel.
3. Notice the sensations you feel in your body.
4. Notice what body parts have more sensation than others.
5. Notice if some muscles start involuntary jumping.
6. Notice if your breathing changes.
7. Notice how long it takes your body to relax more muscles.
8. What else do you notice? Keep noticing and focus on the small, minuscule parts of your body that you may be noticing for the very first time. This is another way

to position your body to feel the energy of your non-physical presence and to practice feeling yourself in this way.

9. Once you've sat long enough with one ankle on top, switch so that the other ankle is on top.
10. Repeat numbers two through eight again, noticing if you feel different with the other ankle on top. What feels different now?

Elijah

Years ago, I briefly dated a man I'll call Elijah. We lived in the same city and liked each other a lot. Then I moved to a different city, and we stopped dating. About five years later while driving home, I noticed a pleasurable feeling in my body every time I was on a specific block. That block was four blocks from my home at the time; I drove on that street frequently to get home. There was also a light at the end of that block, which was often red, so sometimes I stopped on that block for a few minutes, which helped me acclimate to that feeling more. The pleasing feeling came to me every time. The feeling was so pleasing that it stood out and got my attention as I became more aware of it. The intuition in my body was signaling that something on that block was for me.

Shortly after that, I unexpectedly ran into Elijah at a location about thirty minutes away from my home. He had since moved to the same city I was living in. We ended up dating again, and the first time I went to his home, I learned that it was on the block where I got the feeling. That exact feeling didn't persist, but similar feelings continue to appear for me to this day, drawing my attention when I am near something I am meant to experience.

EXERCISE
A Mattress Practice

Purpose: To practice feeling and increase your awareness of your non-physical abundance.

Your connection to Spirit is the life force that gives you energy. The following is a simple practice that you can do at any time:

1. When in bed or on the sofa, stop what you're doing and focus on what you feel. Allow yourself to feel the non-physical energy in and around you as well as the energy of other living things in your presence.
2. Lie on your back.
3. Close your eyes and intentionally relax all your muscles, becoming aware that either the mattress or sofa is holding you up.
4. Let yourself sink in.
5. After about five minutes or less, you will start to notice the subtle non-physical presence that is you. This practice is a great way to feel your non-physical presence, so do this if you ever need to be reminded that it exists or if you want to tune in to your non-physical self more.
6. Once you're more familiar with feeling the energy of your non-physical presence, play a bit. Switch your position and lie on your stomach, then your left side, your right side, and back to your back. Notice the difference in how your non-physical energy feels when in each of those other positions. Compare what your feel,

how much, and where when you lie on one side versus another.

An alternative is to sit in a cross-legged position with one ankle on top of the other, leaning comfortably against a surface. Place your hands on both knees with your palms facing up. Feel the energy around you now. You can also play with this by placing your palms facedown.

REPEAT AFTER ME:
I choose to feel the abundance that I am.

EXERCISE
Sending Your Energy to Physical Locations

Purpose: To practice using your imagination to send your energy.

As an energetic being, you are in constant communication throughout your life via your ability to communicate with the world around you through the multiple forms of energy: mechanical, sound, light, and chemical energy. Energy is constantly transpiring from one energetic location to another, whether it's the traffic you sit in, the food you prepare, the errand you run, the door you hold open, the new friend you make, or the heated exchange with someone you love. It even includes reading these words right now, words that are coming from me, holding my energy in the same way they would if they were verbally spoken from me to you. All of these are variations of managing, shifting, and creating energy.

Let's play with sending your energy to a place you plan to be soon.

1. Think of a place you are planning to be in the near future. It's ideal to select a place that will be uncomfortable for you for whatever reason; this way, you will reap the greatest benefit from this exercise.
2. Then, in this moment, sit in a comfortable seat.
3. Place your bare feet on the floor, lean back, and relax. Close your eyes.
4. With a closed mouth, take long, deep, full breaths.
5. Place both of your hands on your heart chakra.
6. Visualize your energy going from where you are to where you will be.
7. Manage your thoughts by only thinking about what you want to happen in that location. Sit with that for a while until it feels pleasing to you and you are upbeat and energetically attractive.
8. Give your energy a color; it can be any color that feels pleasing to you in this moment.
9. Visualize your colorful energy flowing from one location to the next, engaging your creativity. If the destination is in another country, for example, you might envision a map in your mind's eye and "see" your energy journeying across water and other countries before reaching its destination.
10. Once you "see" your energy arrive, maintain that connection with the destination.

11. Start to feel inside your body. How do you want to feel when you get there? What outcome do you want to achieve?
12. Let the feelings of your desired outcome envelop you, and stay in that space for as long as it feels right for you.

You can also use this practice to allow yourself to receive the energies you want to embody and the ideas and attributes associated with the desires you want to manifest. You can achieve that by allowing yourself to feel what it would be like to have the desire if it were already yours. Use your imagination to envision how you will feel, what you will be doing, what you will be thinking, etc., and then let yourself feel it. Doing this supports the energy that you want to receive making its way to you. For example, suppose you want to be more carefree like the people you met somewhere. In that case, imagining yourself in that place with their carefree attitude will connect you to that carefree energy even though you are not physically there.

Other Examples of How to Energetically Align with the Physical World Around You

- Align with your circadian rhythm by waking when the sun rises and/or intentionally slowing down the rest of your day (or even going to sleep) when the sun sets.
- Count in order when working out or while doing other activities that relate to order.
- Eat more when you are active and less when you are sedentary.

Look for bodily clues that you are more energetically aligned; these will depend on your relationship with yourself and how alignment feels to you based on how often you have felt it. You may feel less constriction in the body (i.e., lowered shoulders, relaxed jaw, etc.), fuller breath, being more easy-going and less moody, clearer thoughts instead of having many thoughts at once, or less jitters and a calmer nervous system.

The feeling of energetic alignment is your energetic home, where you are most comfortable. Sometimes, when aligned, you will receive lots of new energy, which can show up as you doing things quickly and sloppily, dropping things, being nervous or seemingly chaotic, or talking fast. If that happens, empower yourself by breathing deeply and recognizing that you are aligning with new, less-familiar energy. Choose how you manage that energy by becoming as calm as possible.

Lots of new energy may also show up mentally via faster thoughts; you may be thinking from one thing to the next thing to the next. These thoughts will not be random, silly things that don't have an impact, but rather meaningful thoughts that contribute to what you've already been thinking about, as if your understanding is connecting the dots for you. You may resolve significant things you've contemplated for a while in a couple of minutes, enlightening your path of personal growth.

Self-Love Action: Talk to Yourself Out Loud

Enrich the opportunity to better relate to how your body feels by talking to yourself while you soothe your body's stressed, tight, constrictive parts. In these moments, affirm that you are loved and notice the constricted parts of your body start to melt. Speaking lovingly to yourself with purpose lets you hear and receive those messages in your outer ear and has a deeper impact on you. It's one thing to think *I like how I look today* and another thing to say that out loud to yourself. Hearing the affirmation deepens it.

Keep noticing loving thoughts about yourself as they come, and add this out-loud practice. As you keep talking to yourself in this way, it will become easier to find the words, and those words will more easily come out of your mouth. You can also continue this by contributing to conversations with others about yourself and playing up their compliments.

Key Takeaways

- Your body is a primary means of self-communication.
- At any time, you can calm yourself.
- Expanding your awareness of your body's capacity to feel is integral.

Your body serves as a profound medium of self-communication. In any moment, you hold the power to soothe and center yourself. Cultivating a deeper awareness of your body's incredible capacity to feel is essential to accessing more intuition.

Reflection: Find Your Body's Voice

Take a walk. If not now, then later. Walking is a great way to communicate with your body and yourself in general. While walking, give all attention to your body and initiate a conversation with your body by noting the following:

- How does your left leg feel with each footstep?
- Do your feet prefer grass or concrete?
- How do your hands feel?
- What are your arms doing?
- Does your waist want to twist?

- Is your belly loose?
- Are your collarbones spread?
- Which calf feels stronger?
- Are your hips even?
- Do your arms want to stretch?

Make a note of your answer to each question in your journal, or record yourself answering these questions as a voice memo on your cell phone. Feel free to add your own questions.

These are examples of your body's voice. Every action your body takes gives voice to your body. The inner conversations your body has when it is sending and receiving functions naturally happen. Listen for what your body is telling you when you are moving it. For example, your shoulders may tell you when you are uncomfortable. Do you raise them to indicate tension? This is a common constrictive motion, and it happens with other parts of the body too, like curling your toes or tightening your buttocks. Conversely, when you're comfortable, your body releases tension.

The Throat Chakra

The throat chakra, the fifth chakra, is located in the same place as the larynx/voice box. This chakra is associated with the color light blue and signifies your ability to communicate clearly. Effective communication involves passive and active listening. A healthy throat chakra can improve your capacity to listen to your own body as well as external information. Connecting to the throat chakra can enhance your self-communication and expand your ability to listen to the messages your body is sending.

EXERCISE
Connecting with Your Throat Chakra

Purpose: To practice using your energy to support you using your voice when you have something challenging to say.

1. Focus on your throat chakra by thinking of it and bringing as much awareness to it as you can.
2. Hum or swallow, feeling any movement your throat is making as you breathe.
3. Touch your throat with your fingers. Then, notice how you are holding yourself there. Does your throat feel tight, or is it feeling open? That feeling could be due to a cold or inflammation, which is fine; you are just noticing.

Communicating Energy

Let's shift a bit to focus on the communication of your energy. How do you manage the energy you carry? Is this something you think about? Managing energy has to do with your emotions, mood, and attitude as you respond to life's experiences.

A big part of managing your energy is to maintain energetic integrity. Having energetic integrity means not shifting your energy to accommodate someone else only when it is best for you. There is no right or wrong, and you do as you please. We are always learning how to be better communicators in general.

We shift our energy all the time for the benefit of other people, usually without noticing. It's a natural way of connecting with people. I think of it as the adult version of infants who synchronize their heartbeat with their mothers'. However, as adults, it's not always in our best interest to shift energy for others.

The energy you emit is often in response to what is happening in your physical life. Learn to better understand the relationship between your energy and your physical life. This will support you in better managing your energy by giving you more options for understanding your experiences through an expanded perception. That expanded perception gives you more choices about how you want to respond. You also practice energetic integrity by authentically regulating your emotions, mood, and attitude at any given time. If the energy you want to emit is frustration, let it rip.

SEVEN

Set Neutral Intentions

PEOPLE GIVE MORE ATTENTION to what already exists than what is possible. Setting neutral intentions supports your future and is different from an affirmation, which is about the present. Listening to your body helps you create more neutral intentions, which are bountiful and have more options to invite possibility. Your responses to what your intuition shares with you will lead you to realize those possibilities, and realizing possibilities in life is a game-changer.

People can get stuck in their current lives, unable to progress in many ways because they don't think anything else is possible. In actuality, there are multiple routes to living the life they want that enable things to unfold more easily and naturally than the life they're living. Sometimes, we think we know how our lives will progress, and we work so hard to make things happen a certain way that we curtail the possibility of anything else. Setting neutral intentions welcomes unknown possibilities into your life by persuading you to embrace the unexpected, as the intuitive response to living your desired experience may lead you to options you didn't know were possible. By setting neutral intentions, you tap into universal wisdom and allow yourself to receive from the totality of yourself, opening the door to a more fulfilling and abundant life.

Allowing more possibilities in life is a double whammy. Possibilities are freeing and liberating, increasing your awareness of your liberated self by lessening habitual choices. Your intuition will guide you to consider more options than your habitual ones. Setting neutral intentions also connects to seeking inspiration, as you may be spending much of your life operating habitually instead of inspirationally.

Habit and inspiration are on two ends of the spectrum. Habits can be helpful or hurtful and are typically no-brainer responses, as they come naturally to you. Inspiration comes from the Spirit and can put you to work and be transformational. By seeking inspiration, you expand your ability to find inspiration in everything, including unexpected places that might seem uninspiring at first glance. For example, say you buy the same groceries every time you shop or order the same meal from your favorite delivery or takeout spot. What else might you be inspired to eat that you could also like, or that could be better for you, or that could be something your body wants? Explore new options. Regardless of the situation, ask yourself if sticking to your habits serves you well. Sometimes breaking away from habits is more beneficial.

REPEAT AFTER ME:
I surrender to possibilities.

Creating Possibilities

Getting what you want is an ever-expanding journey of listening to and following your intuition. It is a journey of living the experiences you create, which then creates the desire for new and different experiences. Creating possibilities so you can get to the new is a whole thing in and of itself. One way to create space for possibility is to find the lessons in life's experiences. Sadness, anger, and other difficult emotions offer lessons that enrich us, like fertilizer being added to soil.

EXERCISE
Finding the Lesson

Purpose: To create space for possibility.

When you are faced with a difficult experience, consider the following.

Reflect on the experience. Take time to think about the experience or situation you're dealing with. Consider what happened, how you felt, and what the outcome was. Reflection helps you gain clarity and understand the context of the experience.

Identify the key elements. Break down the experience into its key components. What were the significant events or decisions? Who was involved? What were your actions and reactions? Understanding these elements helps you pinpoint what part of the experience holds a valuable lesson.

Ask insightful questions. Challenge yourself with questions like:

- What did this experience teach me about myself or others?
- What could I have done differently, and what did I learn?
- How can this experience help me grow or change?
- What strengths or skills did I discover or develop through this experience?

Look for patterns. Reflect on if this experience connects to other situations or patterns in your life. Are there recurring themes or lessons that are coming up for you? Recognizing patterns can provide deeper insights and guide you in addressing similar challenges in the future.

Extract positive lessons. Focus on the positive takeaways from the experience. Even if it is difficult, there are often lessons about resilience, adaptability, or personal growth. Identify these lessons and consider how they can be applied to improve your future actions or decisions.

Create an action plan. Use the lessons learned to develop a plan for moving forward. What changes can you make based on this new understanding? How can you apply these insights to future situations or goals?

Stay open and curious. Keep an open mind by remaining curious about your experiences. Sometimes, the lessons take time to be clear, but being willing to learn can help you uncover valuable insights.

By consistently recognizing and appreciating the value that life lessons bring, you can turn even the most challenging experiences into opportunities for growth. Integrating these qualities will move you into a happier emotional state, and your body will follow. You will expand your body's ability to feel good in new places that your intuition can travel to, and share possibilities.

Choosing Neutral Intentions

Please note that you can be neutral in attitudes, words, deeds, or actions. Intentions connect to what you allow yourself to think, as they are deposited in your subconscious mind, and your subconscious will draw on them as needed. Being neutral requires conscious attention to a lifetime of conditioning that affects your subconscious thoughts and feelings. Neutral intentions represent your aspirations and what you want more of. They are open-ended and expand your possibilities, fostering more freedom, time, love, health, wealth, adventure, etc.

You can also be fixed in your intentions. Being mindful of your neutral and fixed intentions helps you understand how to control your habits better. Fixed intentions represent what you don't want more of in your life. Fixed intentions are close-ended and restrictive, and they limit possibilities. Being fixed comes from fear of reliving unwanted experiences and is a controlled response to manage emotions. It's helpful to reflect on the outcome of past experiences when you had a fixed intention; consider how that intention impacted potential outcomes and led you to reap lesser benefits.

One helpful way to notice when you are being fixed is to look out for negative self-talk and counter it. When you counter fixed intentions, you shift from only creating what you have experienced to allowing what you desire to begin happening.

Identifying where you are neutral and fixed also helps you become less judgmental. Like judgment, the threat of being fixed is that it doesn't allow other possibilities. It may keep you from noticing all the opportunities that could lead to manifesting your desires. For example, you may have a fixed intention of how life will progress from point A to B and eventually C. But, if you have a neutral intention about how you get from point A to point C, you may not need point B at all!

EXERCISE
Neutral and Fixed Intentions

Purpose: To practice changing your thinking.

Although neutral intentions are preferable, your intentions may go back and forth between being neutral and fixed, which is normal! You are likely to be more of one or the other when it comes to specific areas of your life or topics where you have had more unpleasant, hurtful, or painful experiences. The goal is to talk yourself forward into your most expansive intention in real time.

1. When you notice that you are being fixed, be easy with yourself and remind yourself that there is always more than one way.
2. Use that moment by turning it into appreciation. Appreciate the opportunity to push past fixed intentions and open more possibilities by thinking about what else.

3. Acknowledge that you have done so and mentally thank yourself. Doing so supports you subconsciously by aiding in changing your thoughts and sparks the creation of more new thoughts.
4. Be expectant of your desires in your neutral intentions (and in life!). Know that your desires are on the way to you. Let that knowing reflect in your emotion, mood, and attitude about what you desire. Being expectant helps you be more neutral. Expectancy is a state of being, and it includes your intentions, desires, and manifestations. Plus, it solidifies intentions so that they materialize in the physical world.
5. Counter your fixed intention by creating a neutral intention. It doesn't matter if you don't believe the neutral intention; over time, you will come to believe it. For example, instead of saying, "I hope to find the love of my life," you could say, "The love I've always wanted is coming into my life." Do you notice the difference? You can be even more expectant by saying something like, "The love I've always wanted is so close I can feel the beat of their heart!"

EXERCISE
A Lights-Out Chant

Purpose: To practice planting neutral intentions in your subconscious mind.

A great time to practice neutral intentions is when you're in bed with the lights off, preparing for sleep. Sleep connects you to your subconscious mind, so as you prep for bed in other ways (like brushing your teeth, taking a shower, or putting on an overnight face mask), add a repetitive neutral intention to your nighttime routine.

1. Before beginning your nightly routine, reflect on a fixed intention you had today.
2. Then, take a moment to think of a neutral intention instead.
3. Adjust your emotions, mood, and attitude accordingly.
4. While you wash your face, body, and/or hair as part of that routine, repeat your neutral intention aloud.
5. As you enter your bedroom, begin to mentally repeat your neutral intention to yourself.
6. Continue to repeat as you drift to sleep.

A Story of Two Strangers

My youngest nephew has been going to the barbershop since he could walk. One day when he was four years old, he and his dad arrived for a scheduled appointment with his usual barber. The second my nephew walked in the door, he headed straight to the back of the shop, where a man he had never seen before was sitting alone in a chair. My nephew hugged him, and the man reached down to hug him back. My nephew stayed there for a few minutes, laying his head near the man's shoulder. The hug lingered. Then, the man started crying. All the other men in the shop stopped and watched the exchange between the two, as the sobbing caught the attention of those who were not already paying attention. When the man stopped crying, he shared that he had been going through a really rough time and was so grateful for the hug because he needed that moment of support. My nephew's intuition knew, and the man (subconsciously) allowed the possibility of receiving unexpected support from a stranger.

A Friendship Story: Kenya

Years ago, my friend Kenya visited me at my home. She stopped in the entryway to look at the old family photos I had on the wall. One picture was a black-and-white photo from the 1960s of three rows of thirty-one men, all dressed in Freemason outfits with hats to match.

Kenya asked who was in the picture. I told her my grandfather was. She looked at the picture closely, scanned all the faces, and then pointed him out. "It's him," she said, and she was accurate.

I have three grandfathers, and the man in that photo was not my biological grandfather. He and I look nothing alike. He raised my mom and was the father of her two brothers, but we were not genetically related.

Kenya wasn't surprised that she knew, and neither was I. She was just being herself! Kenya is one of those people in my life who I am deeply connected to, and it shows up in unusual ways. When she took an interest in my family photos, her intuition unexpectedly came to the forefront.

This sort of knowing between us goes both ways. For example, about five years later, my intuition told me Kenya was pregnant even though we had not contacted each other in about four months. Who knew connections in friendships could show up like this?

Self-Love Action: Find Your Sweet Spot

Your sweet spot is like your North Star, a reference point guiding your progress in life. Finding your sweet spot means knowing what responses are best for you. This is helpful to know as you allow yourself to set neutral intentions. In this way, you will stay open-minded to possibilities and respond favorably to whatever is happening.

Your sweet spot might be what you are naturally good at, the skill you like to use the most, or something you have a clear understanding of. Your sweet spot may also be a form of self-expression where you have exceptional talent or even something you don't like that comes easily. Maybe your sweet spot is something you overlook because it's so natural that you don't consider it special, but other people do, and they tell you so.

To discover your sweet spot, ask yourself, *What personality traits and characteristics serve me best for navigating my life?* You will find your sweet spot somewhere in that answer.

Your sweet spot guides you via a sense of peace. Like a game of "hot or cold," you get closer to your destination when you feel at ease. You can be anywhere physically yet maintain groundedness when you operate from that space.

Key Takeaways

- You have the power to create possibilities.
- Embracing neutrality unlocks a world of opportunities that resonate with your desires, waiting to be discovered.
- Nurture your subconscious mind to align with your deepest desires.

You possess the incredible power to create endless possibilities. By embracing a state of neutrality, you open the door to a realm of opportunities that deeply resonate with your innermost desires. Nurture your subconscious mind and allow it to align harmoniously with your truest aspirations. Embrace this journey and watch as your dreams transform into reality.

Reflection: Checking In with Your Non-Intuitive Perception

Checking your perception is a crucial detail in setting intentions and managing the reality you're creating in a healthy way. It's essential not to make something mean something when it doesn't. For instance, the phenomenon of seeing 1111 and other similar numbers has gained popularity in pop culture, as they are often perceived as "angel numbers." However, as unique as the number 1111 may seem, it is also a time; like many other numbers, it will appear twice daily. Thus, seeing this number is not always your intuition. Only some things are guidance or information from your intuition, while some things are simply a part of life. When you see that number (or any other), it is not necessarily intuitive guidance—sometimes, it is just the time.

Seeing angel numbers is just one example of how your perception is critical as you engage more with your intuition. Intuition's ability to challenge your existing perceptions and life experiences is the most fascinating demonstration of your growth on this journey, and this connects to why checking in on your perception is essential: You don't want to make things up. You naturally receive more than enough guidance. Checking in with your non-intuitive perception will help you manage your intuitive perception.

Here are some examples of ways you can check your perception in everyday life.

Reflection: The next time you have a challenging day at work or a stressful encounter, take a few moments to reflect on how you're feeling and why. For instance, if you had a tough meeting, ask yourself if you view the situation as a personal failure or a learning opportunity. Reflection can help you adjust your perception and approach future challenges with a more balanced awareness.

Goal Setting: Regularly assess your personal goals and progress toward your achievements. If you set a goal to improve your fitness and find yourself frustrated with slow progress, checking in with your perception might involve recognizing the small victories along the way and adjusting your expectations. For instance, you could break your fitness goal into smaller, more manageable milestones and celebrate each milestone as a victory. Setting goals can help you stay motivated and adjust your perception of progress.

Engage in Self-Compassion: When you make a mistake or face a setback, it's not just about acknowledging the error but also about being kind to yourself. For example, if you miss a deadline, instead of rebuking yourself, recognize the mistake, understand what you can learn from it, and give yourself credit for the effort you've put in. The practice of self-compassion is a crucial part of managing your perception and fostering mental well-being, providing you with the support and encouragement you need.

Regular Self Check-Ins: Set a routine for regular self check-ins, like a weekly review of your emotional state and life satisfaction. Ask yourself questions like, "How do I feel about my current situation?" or "What parts of my life am I most content with?" Self check-ins can help you stay aware of your perception and adjust as needed.

The Third Eye Chakra

The third eye chakra is the most well-known chakra, so much so that there are even memes about the third eye. Your third eye chakra is smack-dab in the center of your forehead. It is associated with the color indigo and helps you perceive beyond ordinary sight, typically referred to as "seeing beyond the veil." Imagine a veil being placed over your physical eyes, obstructing and preventing clear sight. With this chakra, you can "see" beyond physical sight, as this kind of sight refers to awareness, emotion, and perception, making this chakra a valuable intuitive tool in understanding intuition and ensuring accuracy.

The third eye chakra has the ability to understand non-physical life. It is a highly active chakra; every time you picture or envision something in your mind's eye rather than your physical eyes, you tap into your third eye. Some people worry that their third eye chakra is "blocked." If you can visualize anything, then your third eye chakra is not blocked. With that being said, not all of us use the third eye chakra in the same way. Since intuition is spiritual and connects to non-physicality, it is many things and can express itself in countless ways. The third eye chakra essentially assists us in having experiences we didn't imagine possible. Be open to the surprises of how you use yours. For example, I use my third eye chakra every time I share a clairtangent reading, as a lot of what I share I envision in my mind's eye. As intuition is an abstract mode of receiving accurate information, using intuition is a progression of knowing yourself and your natural abilities as a human being to assist you in better navigating life. This chakra is the apex of that.

EXERCISE
Connecting with Your Third Eye Chakra

Purpose: To invite an opening.

This exercise is designed to help you tap into your third eye, activating its functions. These functions will be unique to you and are associated with your intuition and the manifestation of your desires. In this exercise, you will focus on your individual desires and learn to envision them in your mind's eye.

Do this morning or night, and choose the time of day that works best for you. If you do this exercise in the morning, you can go about your day with a focused awareness, making choices that align with your desires. If you do this exercise at night, your desires will likely make themselves known to you in your dream state, which is a sign of their attainability because they are embedded in your subconscious. Whether you're a morning or night person, this exercise can be tailored to fit your schedule, and committing to this practice will help your desires manifest.

1. Find a quiet place. If there are not any accessible quiet places, wear headphones and play instrumental music (music with words will be distracting).
2. Sit or lie in a relaxing position. You will be still for a prolonged period of time, so be mindful about your body's unique needs. Have pillows and blankets with you, and position yourself with those items if needed.

3. When you are ready, think of a desire that is personal to you. Next, use a neutral intention to express that desire.
4. Then, put all of your attention on your third eye. Do this by closing your eyes and taking your inner gaze up, as if you are looking at the center of your forehead and a bit cross-eyed. Keep your eyes closed. Initially, this may feel weird or a little uncomfortable, but you will get used to it.
5. With your mouth closed, begin to consciously breathe by sending your breath to your third eye. Simply imagine it happening. You can send your breath to any place in your body to create a more energetic space.
6. Imagine your breath expanding your third eye chakra. Maybe you visualize your forehead expanding or the color indigo swirling around. Do whatever works for you.
7. As you exhale, mentally state your neutral intention and expand it by including a form of positive self-talk, chant, or prayer at the end.
8. Add to your neutral intention by imagining, thinking, and envisioning yourself living that desire. (Envision yourself by recognizing your role, purpose, and how you relate to others and your environment beyond how you do so now.) Allow your mind to explore every aspect of this fulfilled desire. Picture the specific details of your desired reality: See the colors, textures, and surroundings. Think through how it would change your daily routines, relationships, and sense of self. While gazing up and cross-eyed at the center of your forehead,

repeat your neutral intention while exhaling to connect it with your breath.

9. Expand upon your imagination of your neutral intention by feeling the emotions and sensations you would experience; hear the sounds and conversations that would fill this new life. Engage all your senses as you see yourself not just having achieved this desire, but actively living within it as your natural, everyday reality.
10. Begin to add visualization by mentally envisioning yourself living your desire in this chakra.
11. Do this for as long as you are able.

I recommend making this exercise a part of your daily routine.

EXERCISE
An Indigo World

Purpose: To further crystallize the desired thought with the desired outcome.

You can also do this less-intense visualization exercise as needed to help you set neutral intentions by connecting with the third eye chakra.

1. Come into your mental space by thinking about the space at the center of your forehead. Then, affirm to yourself, "I have arrived at my third eye chakra."
2. Think of the color indigo to represent that mental space. Then, visualize your thoughts in the color indigo however you'd like. For example, you could visualize the

color outlining your forehead or your forehead itself in that color, or you could envision the whole scenario in the color indigo, including people and places. Do whatever feels most pleasing to you.

3. Sit comfortably in any position with your visualization of an indigo world for at least fifteen minutes. Let it play out like a movie.

EIGHT
Allow New Perspectives

THERE'S A LEARNING CURVE to overcome. Once you set neutral intentions, you automatically begin to allow new perspectives. Allowing new perspectives means permitting yourself to experience life beyond what you have already experienced, and there is so much in life that you have not yet experienced.

A New You

Allowing new perspectives is transformational, and you may need to give yourself permission to do that. In the process, you will create a healthier, more available, non-physical version of yourself that allows more of your intuition to be accessed. As your life unfolds, you will feel more confident and safe in your choices, and the benefits of being different than how you were before will be evident.

Examples of Allowing Intuition

- Expand and express your emotions, thoughts, and ideas to interact as much with your inner world as they do with the outer world. Speak and share freely; what you have to share is valuable. This is especially helpful for sensitive types who have a harder time speaking up. Recognize that being sensitive is a gift and a strength with lifelong benefits; you simply need to learn how to manage your sensitivities more effectively so that your sensitive nature works more in your favor.
- Have fun with new experiences simply because they are new, and enjoy all that comes with newness.
- Become more sensual by enlivening the use of your five senses. Have a greater appreciation for what you touch, taste, hear, smell, and see. Remind yourself that you have these senses, and indulge in your use of each.
- Increase your confidence in your non-physical self's ability to support you by keeping a journal that documents when sensitivities show up via pleasurable and unpleasurable sensations. Also, note when you recognize that you are becoming more sensitive. For example, if you eat a multivitamin gummy every day, one day you may notice that it's way too sweet or sour for you now when previously it was not.
- Embrace the unknown. Initiate alternative thoughts about how something can happen and how you respond to any situation.

The point of allowing intuition is to create change that brings more joy into your life. Allowing new perspectives leads to that change by better aligning you with more of your Spirit to surrender to your new way of experiencing life. You'll begin to adopt a bird's-eye view of current life experiences and receive greater insight into why the expanded perception is more accurate for you.

A Remote Clairtangent Reading

Even though I've been sharing clairtangent readings since 2012, my ability to do so always blows me away. During a reading with a client, I received a vision of tree bark in my mind's eye (clairvoyance) that was around the perimeter of the client's heart chakra in the shape of a heart. I told the client I noticed tree bark in different colors and textures, which is how I knew it was more than one kind of bark. I also shared that this was unusual, because I usually pick up people when focused on the heart chakra, either the client themself or their loved ones. I asked the client if tree bark was significant.

The client said yes and shared that recently, she and her grandmother were in her backyard. The client had asked her grandmother where she should plant a tree, and the two had been looking at different types of tree bark. The client then shared that her grandmother had since passed away. She said she missed her grandmother and had been feeling overwhelmed with sadness. Her love for her grandmother presented itself in the heart chakra, not as the grandmother herself, but as tree bark, which was unusual for how I typically receive information in my readings.

The distinctive nature of this reading stood out to me, representing my ability to allow new perspectives through the expanded perception of the tree bark in a place on the body I did not expect to receive that information, which communicated to me that it connected to something meaningful for my client.

EXERCISE
Allowing Intuition

Purpose: To practice accessing more intuition.

Allowing intuition requires thoughtful input, thoughtful in the intentionality of how you're being to help shift an experience from your subconscious to conscious, allowing you to access intuition. When your self-communication has led you to an outcome or an idea about any area of your life, use this exercise to tap in to your intuition.

1. Calm yourself. Stop whatever you're doing and focus on your breath. Begin to take longer, slower breaths with seven-second inhales and seven-second exhales. Deep breathing is calming.
2. Perform a head-to-toe scan. Mentally scan your body to notice if you are holding any tension. If so, continue breathing to release that tension as needed.
3. Trace your intuitive path. Mentally, go through all the activities that led you to your intuitive guidance. Think of it as tracing the path of your intuition. If it began as a sign in your outer world, ask yourself what that sign connects to. If it started with a feeling in your inner world, locate that feeling in your body. Think of the feelings you locate in your body as landmarks.
4. Connect the dots. Take deeper breaths than usual. While your body is relaxed and tension-free, think about and recall how you intuitively guided yourself.
5. When you're done, reassure yourself that you trust yourself and thank yourself for receiving your intuition.

Say, "I'm grateful for my ability to support myself, and I thank myself for being wise beyond my knowing."

Shifting Self-Perception

Much of allowing new perspectives involves simply valuing yourself differently. This value is in the experiences of your inner and outer worlds: What are you capable of when you balance engagement with both? Changes in self-perception will occur in your inner world first, so you may not notice them initially or give yourself credit for your hard work. Pay attention to changes occurring in your patterns of awareness, feelings, thoughts, attitudes, words, deeds, actions, ideas, etc. The changes can be abstract and may take some time for you to process. Even though change implies action, that action happens in your inner world. Everything else that needs to happen will follow that lead.

One abstract example of change could be your sleeping patterns, as you may notice you suddenly need more sleep than usual as you are processing more. The physical manifestations of your shifting self-perception may also show up in unexpected ways; for example, you could start feeling more of your presence in your body and any room. Another way to recognize your self-perception is shifting is by understanding something familiar in a different way than you ever have before. One major shift will be knowing that you are never alone; your expanded consciousness will demonstrate that your intuition proves the presence of Spirit in and around you.

It's important to know that your reality truly shifts when you are not intentionally connecting to Spirit. You'll notice change while doing the same old, same old activities in your life. Gently, subtly, the newness of an experience will flow to you. In those mundane moments, you will realize that all of life is divine, even when you are not engaged in spiritual activities.

Your perspective of yourself and your life will change before your situations and circumstances do. The severity of change will depend on how much of your life you live in alignment with your true self. The closer you are to being aligned, the less there is to change, although you will continually expand. As you have new desires throughout your life, each will require something to change to allow for expansion and alignment with your new desire. If you find yourself having a hard time allowing yourself to change, encourage yourself with positive self-talk in the same way you would encourage a close friend.

Abundance and expansiveness can be uncomfortable for some. Even though they are tied to experiences you want to have, they will be new in some ways, and newness can be temporarily uncomfortable. As your reality shifts, you will feel different, contributing to the discomfort. In those instances, push through the old—whatever it is—to accept the new being presented to you. Working through the discomfort of the new requires ongoing reminders that you trust yourself and your new way of understanding, experiencing, thinking, and responding. You will learn to find relief as you trust yourself more. Remember, you can choose to trust yourself more at any time. Eventually, the feeling of newness will please you.

Focus on your happiness and doing what makes you happy. Trust and happiness are deeply intertwined. Satisfaction in the quality of your relationships (including the one with yourself), reducing stress, being social, and resolving conflicts intuitively also bring happiness in ways not typically thought of. Being happy lessens discomforts you may be dealing with while supporting your trust in yourself.

Retrograde-Like Completions

Intuition may guide you full circle, leading you back to complete something you thought was finished. These revisits to past experiences or areas of your life signify progress and forward motion, even if they don't fit the standard definition of progress. It's similar to when a planet is retrograde; planets do not physically move backward when retrograde—they only appear that way from our perspective on Earth. Similarly, shifting your perception will bring about changes in perspective. Embrace these moments as opportunities to complete your past, freeing you to live fully in the present. During these moments, avoid getting caught up in past emotions or habits. Instead, stay focused on the present, being mindful to avoid reliving the past while revisiting it.

Take necessary action. If helpful, take action after slowing down to process and reflect. Action can be mental, behavioral, physical, psychological, spiritual, or emotional. Each leads to changes in thought, feeling, and perception about what you are revisiting.

One of Many Stories

This is an example of one of life's retrograde-like completions. In June 2024, an old friend kept popping into my head. I hadn't communicated with this person in seven or eight years, but I kept seeing their name showing up in multiple places, and the reminders were so obvious that I thought about calling.

Even though my intuitive guidance was strong enough that I thought about calling, I did not pick up the phone. Our relationship had been tumultuous, and the thought of talking to this person brought up negative emotions in me, so I thought it best not to call. I noted that I still had some lingering emotional stuff to work through and focused on that instead.

The same day I made the choice not to call, my old friend sent me a text of an image with a quote. I don't recall the quote exactly, but it was something about doing inner work. I sent a light-hearted reply and then received an immediate phone call.

We had a brief exchange that demonstrated that although I had some residual emotions to work through, I had still grown. During the call, I immediately recognized the old pattern of this person holding me accountable for doing inner work that would lead to them managing our relationship in a way that pleased them.

I became angry with myself for replying because the quote in that text told me all I needed to know. However, I was being friendly. What I tolerated from this person in the past was no longer tolerable. That brief re-engagement pointed me to the personal work I still needed to do regarding setting boundaries. Our conversation demonstrated that this person could not be supportive of me and that my relationship with them was over.

Evolving Through Stillness

New perspectives often arise out of stillness. So, I encourage you to create stillness in your mental space. Unlike the quiet of meditation that creates space, stillness creates presence. Stillness is not limited to physical stillness and can even be achieved outdoors. For many, mental stillness can occur while being active and wholly engaged in any activity. The goal is to focus deeply enough on something that all other distractions are minimized, whether those distractions are in your inner or outer world.

As difficult as stillness can be at times, it is a doorway to hearing from yourself and receiving your intuition. Get in the habit of incorporating the following activities in your daily life to invite stillness.

- Play music that is uninterrupted, meaning it has no commercials or ads.
- When home alone or alone in a room, ensure that the room is totally silent. Turn off everything that makes a sound, including your cell phone. Continue your regular activities in silence.
- Create a kind, positive self-talk statement about yourself. Repeat it when you recognize that you are thinking unkind thoughts about yourself. In time, you'll become so well-versed at speaking kindly to yourself that unkind thoughts will have nowhere to live in your brain.
- *Woosah* is a word some people use as a cue when they need to relax, though you can create your own sound to be used as a stillness cue. After making your stillness sound, add a neutral intention and hold that space instead of making it fleeting.
- Prolong your immersion in stillness. Write "woosah," "ease," "breathe deep," or something else in places where you will see the note regularly. For example, you could write on a sticky note and adhere to your bathroom mirror or create a colorful graphic to use as your cell phone's wallpaper.

Being still diminishes the false self that connects to your unkind, untrue thoughts about yourself. This part of yourself holds you hostage for whatever hurtful behavior you have caused yourself and others, and it is where the negative inner conversation comes from. The false self appears in your thoughts before it is acted upon. The goal is to find your center. Stillness centers you. Stillness brings you closer to your true self, where your neutral attitude thrives. Being centered will free you from doubt and negative self-talk. Being centered means finding a balance between what you desire and knowing you can attain it, and that's the place where you want your awareness to be.

REPEAT AFTER ME:
I connect to myself through stillness.

Self-Love Action: Lend Meaning to Your Quest

Intuition shows us who we get to be in this life, fulfilling the heart's faint longing for why we exist, what life is about, and the meaning behind experiences. You have a purpose—we all do. Self-assessments, personality quizzes, and questionnaires are no replacement for you leading your life with purpose, guided by intuition. With intuition, you need nothing more than yourself to realize you came to Mother Earth to actualize whatever you want through learning the truth of who you are.

Many of the world's great philosophers teach that the universe sees itself through our eyes and learns about itself through our life experiences. This is what connects you to the Creator, making you the co-creator of your life. You can have whatever you want because life wants to experience itself through you. Keep that awareness.

Key Takeaways

- Concentrate on experiences you have yet to encounter.
- Engage your five primary senses more fully than you currently do.
- Allow your perception to evolve.

Embrace the adventure of experiences still waiting for you. Immerse yourself in the richness of your five senses, allowing their wonders to unfold fully. Give yourself permission to let your perception expand and evolve, opening your mind and heart to the beauty around you.

Reflection: Spend a Day in Gratitude

Pick a day to spend in gratitude. Spending a day in gratitude refers to your personal life, not what you want changed in the world. Your individual consciousness impacts the world, and you can affect collective consciousness by being clear about your life first. Expressing gratitude can be done via your thoughts, attitudes, words, deeds, and actions. Being grateful actualizes the energy that comes with it, allows greater ease, improves your mood, and minimizes stress, making you more receptive to intuitive guidance. When you are grateful, it expands into more gratitude. For example, gratitude can shift you from a place of frustration to one of growth.

Note the current time, and for the next twenty-four hours, allow yourself to be grateful for every experience in your life without needing to experience it in a certain way. It is ideal to start this exercise in the morning and continue throughout the day, but if it is the afternoon or evening, practice spending the rest of day in gratitude and pick it up again for part of the next day.

As you go about your day, dismiss the need to have more of something, including time. Practice gratitude for everything in your life exactly as it exists right now. For example, as you get dressed for your day, be grateful for your ability to do that. Be grateful for being able-bodied enough to exercise, or for the nail salon having a color you like, or for having taste buds as you enjoy lunch, or for being a quick thinker, or for getting your hair steamed—whatever you are doing, you can be grateful for it. Make yourself grateful for everything, including every person you come in contact with, and be sure to be grateful for life overall.

Spending a day in gratitude also includes being grateful for things that annoy you or things that you want to change. For example, if you woke to an unpleasant sound outside your window, instead of being annoyed, you could immediately direct your attention to something you get to do that day. If you are experiencing a hardship, instead of wishing the hardship away, you could give it more attention by thinking about how you want that hardship to work out in a way that pleases you. This is not about resigning yourself to your current circumstances with an "It is what it is" mindset. Rather, you are embracing gratitude for what you have now, knowing it will change. Something more harmonious will present itself. In your personal life, if you have been working to change something but there still have not been noticeable shifts, you have yet to grasp something in that experience. This exercise will help. Being grateful for whatever is happening will help change occur faster.

Even if life feels exceptionally challenging at the moment, be grateful for the gift of life, for every breath, and for the opportunity to experience life as a human being. Wherever you choose to start, you will discover that you have more to be grateful for than you realize.

Note that certain areas of your life may require more or less of your gratitude. Stay aware of the areas in your life where you easily accessed gratitude versus the areas that need more gratitude. Ask yourself why this may be.

You could spend a day in gratitude specifically regarding a certain area where you want to understand yourself more. For example:

- Spend a day in gratitude with your intuition.
- Spend a day in gratitude with your inner world.
- Spend a day in gratitude with your self-love.
- Spend a day in gratitude with your chakras.
- Spend a day in gratitude with your body.

Then, generally reflect on the experience. What was it like to spend twenty-four hours in gratitude? What was the most challenging part of remaining grateful? Did you experience anything surprising? Would you do it again? Can this be a new self-love routine?

The Crown Chakra

The crown chakra, the last of the seven main chakras, is a beacon of divine wisdom. Located at the top of the head and associated with the color violet, it represents divine connection and higher consciousness. This chakra connects you to all earthly and cosmic entities, including angels, ancestors, Spirit guides, and archetypal energies from multiple cultural pantheons. It's like an invisible umbilical cord connecting human beings to their spiritual mother, just as a baby connects to its physical mother. This chakra is a source of support and nurturance from the spiritual world, supporting the awareness of being one with the Divine and opening pathways to profound and enlightening divine wisdom.

EXERCISE
Connecting with Your Crown Chakra

Purpose: To feel your connection to the Divine.

1. Sit in a relaxing position.
2. Close your eyes and focus on your breath until you notice that you feel more relaxed than when you started.
3. Open your dominant hand so that all five fingers are straight.
4. Hold the palm of your dominant hand just above the top of your head, right above the center. Do not physically touch your head.
5. Notice the energy you feel.
6. Acknowledge that feeling as the Divine. The Divine is not far above you in the sky. It is omnipresent and is always right next to, in front of, and around you.
7. Switch hands and do it again.
8. Notice the difference in the feeling with each hand. That difference in feeling is a small indication of the variation of feelings that connecting with the Divine gives you.
9. If you want, do this exercise again, but touch the top of your head this time. Notice if you feel a difference.

NINE

Apply What You Already Know

AMERICAN CULTURE HAS POPULARIZED phrases that make us believe life is supposed to be hard: "No pain, no gain." "What doesn't kill you makes you stronger." "Nothing worth having ever comes easy." Then there's "Life sucks, then you die." That one is just brutal. Many commonly accepted perspectives can hold us back from accessing what we already have within us. These views often prevent us from tapping into the knowledge and insights that exist in the subconscious or conscious mind.

When we hear these phrases from people we love and respect, like family members or friends, we often adopt these ideas without question. However, with the teachings in this book, you are now ready to challenge these beliefs. While outer-world sources say life is hard, intuition tells you life is inspiring and connected in ways that teach you who you are while aligning with what you desire. This makes life an awe-inspiring experience no matter what is going on because you always have yourself to follow first. You have to know that you are your most prized possession. You have the power to enjoy, cherish, appreciate, explore, and live life to the fullest, even with all its hardships; please take full advantage of that.

REPEAT AFTER ME:
I got this.

When it comes to how you experience your life, intuition is not a matter of either/or, but a yes/and proposition; inspiration is always within reach even in the face of challenge. Ebbs and flows of life's joys and pains have positioned you to welcome your intuition. Remind yourself that life is naturally complex; it is joyous and challenging, comfortable and uncomfortable, easy and hard. These highs and lows can last a long time or shift in a matter of hours. We are all in constant transition as we move from one phase of life to another. It's in these transitions that you find your resilience, remember who you are, and let your intuitive self show out. Intuition adds steadiness so you can find stability in taking action.

When you choose to allow intuition, the transition will be seamless. Keep listening, following, and doing what brought you to that point. The source leading you is more than wise, beyond an intelligence that we have a word for. You can trust that Spirit is leading you to your desires because that's all intuition knows. This final chapter sets you up to reap the daily benefits of intuition for the rest of your life, starting now.

EXERCISE
Improving One Improves the Other

Purpose: To document areas of your life where intuition can be helpful now.

1. Jot down if your intuition is currently guiding you in the following areas:
   - Your relationships (with self, partner, children, parents, other family members, professional colleagues, etc.)
   - Your home life
   - Your career and/or finances
   - Your social life
   - Your spirituality or religion, if applicable
   - Your health (mental, emotional, physical, and sexual)
   - Any additional areas that resonate with your life
2. Next, building on what you wrote for number one, note how your intuition speaks to you in each area of life.
3. Then, identify where you need support in receiving and allowing your intuition.
4. Ask yourself which areas of your life need your love and attention right now. Start with the area that is heavy in your heart or mind. By happenstance, improving one area of life will improve another area of life, as everything is connected, even when it seems impossible.

5. Tell yourself you want more clarity in the area you are focusing on.
6. Perform a calming exercise from a previous chapter. Pick the one you liked the most and received the greatest benefit from.
7. Then, ask yourself a question that will guide you toward clarity in that area. This question should be juicy and is an opportunity to get really honest about the hard stuff. For example, you could ask, "What will align me with my greatest power?"
8. Finally, look out for the intuitive answer and document how your intuition led you to that answer. I'm not going to tell you how. You have this whole book; refer to it until the pages wear out. Ask yourself what connections you made through nudges, self-trust, self-loving responses, and listening to your body's communication. All is one.

Repeat this exercise as many times as necessary, naturally going from one area of life to another as needed. Keep reviewing the previous steps in this book for guidance, and keep going back to the exercises. You are developing your intuition, and it takes a minute.

Creating Your Desires

Your intuition identifies all subconscious and conscious desires created from your lived experiences. Intuition will then draw on those experiences and bring your attention to things accessible to you, like the people or conversations that will lead you toward actualizing your desires.

You can create desire out of a lived experience. As the exceptional creator that you are, you're already doing it! Your lived experiences demonstrate your ability to create and, simultaneously, are the greatest indication of what you have yet to create. Combined, that demonstration and indication speak to your capability of having whatever you desire. Please reread those last two sentences.

This makes me think of the saying "Use what you got to get what you want." However, in this context, since I don't know what your lived experiences are or which desires you have, I want to be clear about how a lived experience creates a desire. Here are some examples of how a person could use their lived experience to create the desires they want.

- Awareness of pollution in a large city creates the desire to live in fresh air.
- Awareness of spending a lot of time alone creates the desire to be more social.
- Awareness of constantly giving to others creates the desire to have more reciprocal relationships.
- Awareness of a mundane day-to-day life creates the desire to explore spirituality.
- Awareness of living paycheck-to-paycheck creates the desire to have income security.
- Awareness of a lack of creativity creates the desire for more diverse experiences.

Awareness of anything, especially when it is undesirable, instantly creates the desire for an enhanced experience that is more pleasing, and your intuition takes note of it. When you align with your desires, they expand you in multiple ways. You access new thoughts and ideas about yourself and life as a whole as well as new life experiences.

EXERCISE
Using Lived Experience to Create Desire

Purpose: To further prove your exceptionality.

1. Create a list of some of your lived experiences and the associated desires. Make your list at least ten items long. Note that a lived experience can be a thought, feeling, emotion, mood, attitude, etc.
2. Sometimes a lived experience creates new thoughts, feelings, emotions, moods, attitudes, etc., that are restrictive instead of expansive. Restrictive experiences often connect to pain. For example, if you felt hurt by one family member and severed ties with other family members who were not involved, that would be restrictive. Ask yourself if any of the lived experiences you listed have made you adopt a restrictive perspective.
3. Increase your expectations of your desires manifesting by removing attention from anything unwanted. Doing so is rooted in inner self-talk. This topic is so commonly impactful that it needs multiple mentions. For example, whenever you notice yourself thinking about something you don't want, gently redirect your train of thought.
4. For each restrictive lived experience you identified in number one, consciously reframe it. Ask, "How can this

experience become a source of wisdom, compassion, or strength?" Write down the expanded perspective for each restrictive experience.

5. Review your list of desires and examine whether they stem from a genuine inner calling or from external pressures, fear, or trying to prove something. Circle the desires that feel truly aligned with who you are becoming.
6. Write connecting statements like "Because I experienced [lived experience], I now desire [desire created], which will allow me to [positive outcome]." This helps you see how your past informs your authentic future.
7. For your circled, created desires, write two to three concrete actions you can take. This bridges the gap between subconscious work and conscious manifestation. This creates a complete cycle from awareness to transformation to manifestation to integration as you apply what you already know.

If you like this process and want to take this exercise further, you can continue as follows:

8. Schedule weekly or monthly check-ins to revisit this list, noting which desires are manifesting, which have evolved, and what new lived experiences are shaping your expanding awareness.
9. When you notice yourself naturally thinking from expanded rather than restrictive perspectives, consistently acknowledge it. This reinforces your growth and builds momentum for continued transformation.

Live in Harmony with Your Better Half

Learning to use your intuition changes everything, as it creates more harmony. Receiving intuition is only half of the equation—using intuition is the other half. Receiving is connected to allowing; however, there's a slight but essential difference between the two. Receiving is the natural consequence of acceptance that happens subconsciously, whereas allowing is permission, which is a conscious act. Allowing is a choice between letting intuition remain subconscious (and reaping little benefit) or consciously using this incredible gift. You are in highly skilled hands—hands that are your very own! Remind yourself of that. Your intuition is incapable of misguiding you, and you cannot make a mistake.

Working to manage yourself harmonizes you with your most loving self. Your most loving self will always steer you appropriately, even when you're going through low points. Take consistent, ongoing action to reinforce your awareness of your inner intelligence. As often as needed, repeat to yourself, "I receive myself." Embed that message into your subconscious mind to support you in achieving and sustaining harmony. This is the ultimate affirmation. By now, I hope you know that some part of you is listening and responding. That part is your true better half.

Here are some concepts to revisit once you have built more trust with your intuition. Reflect on these themes to recognize what intuitive messages await you.

- Cosmic and celestial associations, i.e., planets, stars, sun, moon, sky, etc.
- Oceans, rivers, lakes, and other natural water sites
- Cultural references, including ones from outside your native culture that you relate to

- Historical references. Think big. If it helps, imagine yourself as a king, queen, Goddess, or the like
- Ancient beliefs
- Deities and archetypes

EXERCISE
All the Chakras

Purpose: A recap to remind yourself who the heck you are.

When it comes to the chakras, know that each chakra can support another, as one chakra can initiate another's growth. For example, if you find that you are more aligned with one chakra than another, call on support from that chakra to support the chakra that needs more TLC. Be imaginative; visualize the color of the chakra you are more aligned with glowing in the place of the chakra that needs more support. Eat foods the same color as the chakra that needs more support, or wear more of that color in your clothing. As long as you do these things with intention, they will support you energetically and line up your psyche with maintaining that awareness.

1. If you find yourself having a difficult time aligning with your intuition, remind yourself who you are and how natural the process is. Return to each of the chakra exercises in this book to mentally connect with this energy inside of you. Then, state the following affirmations that correlate with each chakra.
2. To connect with the root chakra, say, "I am aware of all of me." This affirmation will enable you to feel safe in your body.

3. To connect with the sacral chakra, say, "I am one with the Divine Spirit." This affirmation will encourage a sense of belonging and partnership with the non-physical.
4. To connect with the solar plexus chakra, say, "I am the person who knows what is for me." This affirmation will fortify your self-trust and confidence.
5. To connect with the heart chakra, say, "I am love." This affirmation empowers you to respond with compassion and understanding in any situation.
6. To connect with the throat chakra, say, "I am in a loving relationship with myself." This affirmation reinforces loving self-communication.
7. To connect with the third eye chakra, say, "I allow the Divine Spirit to guide me." This affirmation means opening yourself to the wisdom and guidance of the Divine Spirit, which can help you create possibilities.
8. To connect with the crown chakra, say, "I am ever-expanding into what is possible for me to experience." This affirmation invites new perspectives and experiences.
9. Spend time with each of these ideas until you know they are true for you. Give yourself a week to repeat each affirmation daily and pay attention to how your view of yourself shifts. Document the results of this exercise in your journal or via a voice memo.

Conclusion

WHAT IF PEOPLE ACKNOWLEDGED and prioritized intuition as a fundamental spiritual need in the same way we consider the other fundamental physical needs of the body, like water, food, and shelter? If that were the case, we'd all use intuition so much that life would be a completely different experience because of all the beautiful possibilities we would open up to both individually and collectively. Let yourself begin to experience that.

Take all that is within this book and make it your own. The tools you've learned and the exercises you've done are resources and examples to refer to as you discover and incorporate creative ways to become more aware of your intuitive nudge that is always readily available to you. With intuition, you can navigate life's most challenging situations with hope and optimism.

So, now what? What is your next step? Focus on just that: steps, not the outcome. If you tend to be too invested in a specific outcome, this can trip you up. Now you know how to let your life experiences fill in the gaps between where you are and where you want to be.

This is a helpful time to reflect and ask yourself, *How has my understanding of intuition and spirituality matured since reading this book?* What do you attribute that spiritual maturity to? What can you do daily to continue growing and expanding your intuition? What needs to change? Perhaps you need to be more honest with yourself, practice meditation, spend more time alone, start journaling, record your feelings and thoughts, express yourself verbally and artistically, spend time in nature, start gardening, go for more walks, consistently exercise, or something else that helps you connect with yourself. Find your certitude.

Activate your dormant knowledge by stimulating your inner world by reading, learning a new skill, or engaging in more heart-to-heart conversations. Continue to document your experiences and insights, and refer to them as you live an intuitive lifestyle. Continue acknowledging your intuition, expanding your awareness, and allowing yourself to receive guidance. There are no rules. Keep listening, following, and doing what brought you to this point.

What you've learned and experienced while reading this book is not just a record of your growth, it is also a testament to your commitment and progress. Right now is only the beginning of a lifetime of knowing yourself, and the exploration of self is why we all get to live this beautiful life.

Intuitive Healing

You've likely experienced a lot of healing as you've moved through this book. We all have things to heal from. While healing was not the intention of this book, self-healing is a natural consequence of being in your power as you balance the dark/unknown/non-physical/inner/spiritual/subconscious and the light/information/physical/outer/human/conscious aspects of yourself. You don't have to be intentional about intuitive healing, but if you want to focus on intuitive healing, you should choose to be intentional about that focus.

Intuitive healing is a facet of self-healing, and it is the ability to use intuition to heal yourself. However, always seek professional support from a mental health therapist until you are seasoned enough in your relationship with yourself to cultivate a healthier self by bringing more balance to your non-physical and physical selves. When you practice intuitive healing, you will be greeted by a world that is more expansive than you knew existed, and that world keeps expanding. The work involved in healing requires allowing all parts of yourself to be accessed—the parts you know and the parts you didn't know existed. Being attuned to your intuition greatly enhances your inner world, which supports you as you navigate challenges in the outer world.

In the opening of this book, when I said I credit my intuition with my ability to heal myself, what I meant was…intuition saved my life. Healing is that real of a thing, and the depths of intuition's guidance are more extensive than I knew. My trauma was prolonged by not knowing myself well enough to allow intuitive information to make its way to me. For a long time, I overidentified with my physical self and did not give my non-physical self the attention it was seeking.

Know that healing is quite possibly the most courageous thing you can do for yourself. Healing is also hard work. It takes courage to explore unknown depths inside yourself, and work to manage how that depth changes your relationship with yourself and your life.

With the help of my intuition, I have shifted from someone who was so private that I didn't even want to take a picture to someone who tells as many people as will listen about the most intimate parts of myself. Fully trusting your mysterious intuition will lead to surprises about who you are, things that no one else could tell you or that you, or anyone else, could make up.

The End Is a New Beginning

You've reached the end of this book, and what a journey it's been, huh? Reread the introduction and the chapters or reengage with the exercises to access more information about your life.

Enjoy every single morsel of everything you learn going forward, and know that this book is my way of always rooting for you. I'm so proud of you for taking all this in, and I'm so excited for what's to come for you! You are shifting your reality—that is a huge feat, and I can't think of anything more impactful for your life experience.

Have faith in yourself and your journey ahead. Play, have fun, enjoy, and remember that life loves you! As a soulmate friend of mine told me years ago, "You better go get your life."

Be well and take supreme care.

Love infinity,

Eboni

Acknowledgments

THIS BOOK WAS MEANT to be. I had not planned to write a single book in life, let alone two, as I've also written a memoir that will be released sometime near the release date of this one. Over many years, my intuition guided me in very different ways to write both. In this book, you learned the specifics of how I understand and experience intuition, and in the memoir, you will learn my life experiences that resulted in me being here. I want to acknowledge the woman in that story who asked if I would be interested in writing a self-help book. Thank you, Lisa Hagan, for believing in both books. You showed up for me and helped me share my message with the world in more ways than either of us expected. I am grateful, thankful, and appreciative of you.

To Write to the Author

If you wish to contact the author or would like more information about this book, please write to the author in care of Llewellyn Worldwide Ltd. and we will forward your request. Both the author and publisher appreciate hearing from you and learning of your enjoyment of this book and how it has helped you. Llewellyn Worldwide Ltd. cannot guarantee that every letter written to the author can be answered, but all will be forwarded. Please write to:

Eboni Banks
℅ Llewellyn Worldwide
2143 Wooddale Drive
Woodbury, MN 55125-2989

Please enclose a self-addressed stamped envelope for reply, or $1.00 to cover costs. If outside the U.S.A., enclose an international postal reply coupon.

Many of Llewellyn's authors have websites with additional information and resources. For more information, please visit our website at http://www.llewellyn.com.